Coaching:

The Key to Improving Staff Performance

FOUNDED 1870

HV
9470
·L38
1999

ISBN # 1-56991-101-0

8/01 dir
$10.—

About the Authors

Karen Lawson, Ph.D., international consultant, speaker, and writer, is president of Lawson Consulting Group, a Philadelphia-based firm specializing in organizational and management development. Dr. Lawson has extensive consulting and workshop experience in the areas of team development, communication, management, and quality service.

Adapted for the American Correctional Association by **Ida M. Halasz**, Ph.D., who served as the Deputy Administrator of the National Institute of Corrections Academy, U.S. Department of Justice. Currently, as Vice President of Powell International Inc., she provides training and consulting services to public and private sector organizations.

Foreword

Correctional practitioners who have served in the corrections field over the last two decades can attest to the transformation in the training of staff. Seemingly, not too many years ago, training consisted of giving new employees a set of keys, a brief overview of their duties and responsibilities, and then allowing the employees to learn on the job through practical experience. A sink or swim mentality seemed to prevail. As the corrections field changed with new ideology, concepts, and practices, it became apparent that all too often the training of staff was either nonexistent or in desperate need of improvement.

Training was identified as the basis for properly instructing new employees, a means to keep employees aware of procedures and inevitable changes, as well as aiding in improving job performance. Jail administrators, in recognizing the importance of training realized that staffing needs and budgetary constraints, frequently prevented off-site training that may have been desired. Additionally, the value of training on the job could be perceived as an extension of the classroom and as a need for actual application in the field.

Understanding this need was the impetus behind developing and publishing the workbook, *On-the-Job Training: The Key to Staff Success*. This workbook can serve to prepare the training staff in developing on-the-job training for employees.

Captain Robert Lucas
Hillsborough County sheriff's Office

a publication of the
AMERICAN CORRECTIONAL ASSOCIATION
Professional Development Department
4380 Forbes Boulevard
Lanham, Maryland 20706-4322
(301) 918-1800
Fax: (301) 918-1900
http://www.corrections.com/ACA

Introduction

Coaching is a critical skill for today's correctional supervisors and managers. Why is coaching so important? Today's correctional environment has created pressure to do more with less. The key to reducing that pressure is to make the most of your most valuable resource—staff.

The goal of this workbook is to help correctional supervisors, managers, and co-workers coach staff to overcome barriers and improve performance. The workbook's innovative approach to solving performance problems presents an effective coaching model and creative coaching techniques. This approach will help correctional supervisors and managers create a supportive environment and address individual differences, including language, culture, age, and value systems.

Table of Contents

Self-Assessment: How Do I Rate as a Coach?

This self-assessment will help you identify those areas where you can improve as a coach. Remember that your goal is to enhance your existing coaching skills so that you can help your staff be more effective in their jobs.

Use the following scale to rate each statement:

I	I	I	I	I
5	**4**	**3**	**2**	**1**
Strongly Agree	Agree	Not Sure	Disagree	Strongly Disagree

1. Set specific performance standards and expectations for my staff? _____

2. Help staff set their own goals? _____

3. Carefully plan for a coaching session by determining what I want to say and what I want the outcome to be? _____

4. Address specific behavior rather than attitude or evaluative judgments? _____

5. Begin a coaching session by expressing empathy and understanding? _____

6. Use active listening techniques such as paraphrase or restatement to ensure clear understanding between myself and the staff member? _____

7. Give the staff member opportunities to offer suggestions? _____

8. Use open-ended questions to encourage staff to open up and express themselves? _____

9. Demonstrate support by using praise and agreement to reinforce what the staff member says? _____

10. Create an open environment that encourages collaborative, two-way communication? _____

11. Guide staff in a problem-solving
    process rather than tell them what to do?   _____

12. Help staff develop a performance
    improvement plan?   _____

13. Meet regularly with staff to monitor
    their performance improvement efforts?   _____

14. Reward staff for achieving the desired
    results?   _____

15. Explain how what they do fits into
    the "big picture"?   _____

16. Communicate to my staff that I have
    confidence in them and their abilities?   _____

17. Prioritize areas for improvement
    rather than address everything at once?   _____

18. View coaching as one of my most
    important supervisory or managerial
    responsibilities?   _____

19. Show a genuine interest in the staff
    during a coaching session through
    positive, nonverbal behavior?   _____

20. Give positive reinforcement to a staff
    member for improving performance, even
    if the person has not yet met my expectations?   _____

Total Score   _____

Use the following scale to determine your success as a coach.

81—100 You are a top-notch, supportive performance coach.

61—80 Your coaching skills need some fine-tuning.

41—60 You need to focus on a few areas for improvement.

21—40 Improving your coaching skills needs to be a top priority.

0—20 You need to closely examine your basic supervisory or
management practices.

PART I

What Is Coaching?

As correctional organizations continue to grow and change, our workforce will become increasingly empowered and self-directed. Staff will no longer be satisfied with receiving information on a need-to-know basis. They will want to know what the organization's plan is, how they fit into that plan, and whether their performance is meeting organizational goals. To meet these needs, the supervisor's or manager's role must change, too, from the traditional task-assigner to that of a coach and facilitator.

In Part I, we will look at exactly what coaching is, when it should be used, and how it can be supported through staff motivation. In Part II, we'll take a step-by-step look at the coaching process.

Chapter One

FROM SUPERVISOR TO COACH

Chapter Objectives

After completing this chapter, you should be able to:

- Identify the benefits of coaching.
- Define coaching, counseling, and training, and identify situations in which they should be used.
- Identify the traits and skills of effective coaches.

Provide staff with information about performance issues as they occur.

We usually recognize and value the coach's role in the sports arena. But we often fail to transfer the principles and practices of coaching to the organizational "playing field." In today's correctional organization, coaching must become an integral part of the overall performance-management system.

Traditionally, many correctional organizations conducted once- or twice-a-year performance appraisals and issued evaluations that were similar to school report cards. But this approach doesn't provide correctional staff with the ongoing feedback they need to succeed in today's changing correctional workplace.

Today's correctional supervisors and managers can't stop at simply evaluating performance—they need to manage it. That means providing staff with information about performance issues as they occur rather than just once or twice a year. The purpose of coaching in these situations is to improve that performance. And, in some cases, coaching becomes one of the first steps in the process of progressive discipline.

Besides improving performance, coaching also can have a positive affect on staff morale. Correctional supervisors and managers sometimes have difficulty motivating their staff. Many have discovered that coaching is an effective tool for improving staff performance and job satisfaction.

Take a Moment . . .

The first step in moving from being a "supervisor" to a "coach" is to change your mind-set. Using the following chart, list the words you associate with "supervisor" and "coach."

Supervisor	Coach
_____	_____
_____	_____
_____	_____
_____	_____

Supervisors and Coaches: Different Approaches

To illustrate the difference between a traditional supervisor and a coach, consider the following situation:

John has been with the state department of corrections for eight years and in the same position for five of those years. He is a good staff member who does his job and is solid, honest, and reli-

able. Although he meets standards and expectations, including deadlines, John shows no initiative and resists new ideas and new ways of doing things.

In dealing with John, a traditional supervisor might simply ignore the situation. The supervisor may assume that John is perfectly happy with his job and just wants to keep plugging along. At most, a traditional correctional supervisor or manager might talk to John and tell him that he should try new ideas and new approaches.

In contrast, a "correctional coach" recognizes John's potential and takes the time to sit down with him. The coach finds out what John likes about his job and what he might like to do to enhance it. The coach expresses confidence in John's ability to excel and encourages him to seek additional opportunities.

What Is Coaching?

The goal of coaching is to create a change in behavior.

Coaching is an ongoing process designed to help staff members gain greater competence and overcome barriers to improving performance. Coaching is appropriate when a staff member has the ability and knowledge to succeed but performance is not at the level needed. The goal of coaching is to create a change in behavior, to move staff from where they are to where you want them to be. Coaching encourages people to do more than they ever imagined they could.

Two Types of Coaching

There are two different types of coaching: spontaneous, on-the-spot coaching and planned, formal coaching. Both can be effective if done properly. However, many attempts at on-the-spot coaching fail because of the correctional supervisor's or manager's natural tendency to take over. For example, a supervisor who accompanies a parole agent to visit a parolee's worksite may intervene to "save" the situation when she sees the visit is going badly. Instead of intervening, the supervisor could allow the parole agent to deal with the situation and then coach the staff member afterward. Another supervisor may believe he is coaching when he pushes a staff member away from the computer and says, "Here, let me show you." Then the supervisor finishes the job.

These interventions are not coaching—they demonstrate a lack of confidence in the staff member and undermine any further coaching efforts. Good coaching, whether planned or spontaneous, focuses on developing the staff member, not making the supervisor look good.

Coaching Versus Training and Counseling

Coaching differs from training, which is a structured process that provides staff with the knowledge and skills to do job tasks. Coaching also differs from counseling, which is directed at personal issues that are affecting (or have the potential to affect) performance. Very often, counseling involves personal problems, such as marital and family problems, substance abuse, and emotional and psychological barriers. The correctional supervisor or manager should not try to counsel a staff member. He or she should serve as a resource person, directing the staff member to a skilled practitioner for further professional help. Many correctional agencies have employee assistance programs that provide confidential counseling.

Situations That Require . . .

Training

- Change in policies or procedures
- New tools or equipment
- New responsibilities
- Move to new department

Coaching

- Increase in errors
- Missed deadlines
- Meeting only minimum standards
- Untapped potential
- Ability to do better
- Need to fine-tune skills

Counseling

- Chronic tardiness or absenteeism
- Emotional outbursts
- Erratic behavior
- Suspected substance abuse

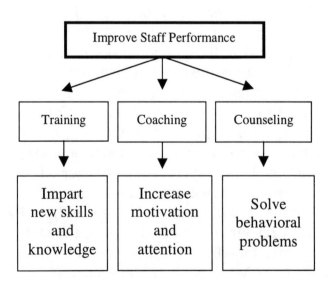

Take a Moment . . .

Identify a staff member whose performance you would like to improve through coaching. You will work with this example as you move through the workbook.

Name:

_____

Situation:

_____

_____

Are you sure that the situation requires coaching—the staff member has the ability and knowledge to succeed but performance is not at the level needed.

☐ Yes

☐ No   If you checked this box, select an individual and situation that fit the criteria for coaching.

That's enough for now; we'll return to this staff member frequently as we move through the workbook.

Benefits of Coaching

Although coaching your staff will take a commitment of your time and effort, it will provide benefits for you as well as your staff.

- **Coaching is the most effective way to develop your staff.** The time you invest will produce long-lasting results.

- **Coaching is the key to managing multiple priorities.** In today's work world of downsizing, cost-cutting, and other

Coaching takes a commitment of time and effort.

changes, correctional supervisors and managers are expected to do more with less. High-performing staff members, developed through coaching, will help reduce the stress of increasing responsibilities and multiple tasks.

- **Coaching leads to improved staff performance,** which leads to increased productivity and bottom-line results. When your staff meet or exceed expectations, everybody wins—you, your staff, and the organization.

- **Coaching increases staff self-esteem and job satisfaction.** People perform better when they feel good about who they are and what they do.

In addition to these benefits, an important reason for coaching is that staff want it. Today's staff are not content with just being told what to do. They need their supervisors' help to excel. This means that your staff expect you to provide them with the tools, techniques, and coaching to succeed.

Staff need their supervisors' help to excel.

Barriers to Coaching

If coaching is such a great approach, why don't more correctional supervisors and managers practice it? The primary barrier to effective coaching can be found within supervisors and managers themselves. Reasons why some supervisors and managers are poor coaches include:

- **They don't know how to coach.** Many correctional staff get promoted to supervisors or managers because they're good at what they do. But they're left to develop their supervisory or management skills through trial and error or modeling the behavior of other supervisors and managers. If they were never coached along the way, they won't know how to do it. This barrier to coaching can be overcome by a variety of training resources, such as this workbook.

- **They don't want to take the time to coach.** No doubt about it, coaching takes time, and that's something most correctional supervisors and managers are short on. But taking the time to coach can save them more time later on. Time management experts have found that for every hour spent planning, three to four hours are saved in execution. The same principle holds true for coaching. Time spent coaching in the short term results in long-term benefits.

- **They don't have the patience to coach.** Some people simply are not patient by nature. But even the most impatient person can develop patience by focusing on the positive outcomes of coaching and practicing it on a daily basis.

- **They believe staff should improve performance on their own.** Many correctional supervisors and managers believe that once a staff member is selected for a job, performance improvement is his or her responsibility—a case of "sink or swim." In some cases, the supervisor or manager may think "I had to learn it the hard way, and if I can do it, so can everyone else." These supervisors and managers need to remember that trial and error is a very inefficient teacher. Staff will perform better and be more productive if supervisors and managers take the time to coach.

Of course, correctional supervisors and managers aren't the only barrier to effective coaching. Staff themselves are often the problem. No matter how skillful or committed the coach may be, coaching cannot succeed unless the staff member is "coachable." Reasons staff might be difficult to coach include:

Explain why change is necessary and how staff can benefit from it.

- **They are resistant to change.** Coaching requires that staff change their behavior, and many people are uncomfortable with change. Some staff members may be so entrenched in their current behavior that they see change—and coaching—as a personal threat.

- **They think they know it all.** Overconfidence sometimes creates a know-it-all attitude. Staff who think they have all the answers will see no reason to change their behaviors and will initially resist coaching efforts.

Staff with these attitudes may be difficult to deal with and supervise. But you *can* overcome both types of staff objections to coaching. Carefully explain the reasons why a behavior change is necessary and describe how the staff member will benefit from it.

Criteria for Success

Successful coaches in correctional organizations, just as those in sports, are great influencers. They know how to bring out the best in others and have a desire to participate actively in each staff member's development. They also know that coaching is an ongoing process and a primary responsibility. They create an environment that empowers groups and individuals to get results.

Being a good coach is a challenge. But it is a challenge that correctional supervisors and managers can meet. The key is to develop the appropriate qualities and skills and translate those into effective coaching traits.

Take a Moment . . .

Identify three situations in which you received effective coaching from someone. These examples can be taken from any time in your life and any type of situation, personal or professional.

Example 1:

_____

_____

Example 2:

_____

_____

Example 3:

_____

_____

Based on these three examples, list below the qualities, traits, or skills that you think an effective coach must have.

1._____   2. _____

3._____   4. _____

5._____   6. _____

7._____   8. _____

9._____   10. _____

Traits and Skills of Effective Coaches

Studies show that effective coaches share certain personal traits, including:

- **Patience**—Successful coaches show patience and understanding. They realize that behavior change takes time and performance improvement happens incrementally.

- **Enthusiasm**—All good coaches are enthusiastic, and they show it. If you have any doubts, just watch the sidelines at a football or basketball game. The coaches are excited, and their enthusiasm becomes contagious. Imagine the results if the great football coach Vince Lombardi had said to his team in a matter-of-fact tone: "Well, you know, guys, it's your job to get out there and win. Give it your best shot."

- **Honesty and integrity**—Effective coaches are noted for their forthrightness and high principles. People follow effective coaches because they do the right thing.

- **Friendliness**—To be a successful coach, you need to draw people to you. An unfriendly demeanor will discourage others from seeking your help or receiving your coaching.

- **Genuine concern for others**—Successful coaches truly care about people and demonstrate their concern through words and deeds.

- **Self-confidence**—To coach others successfully, you must have confidence in yourself. You must believe that you know what you're doing is correct and that you can offer sound guidance to others.

- **Fairness**—The ability to treat people fairly is a quality that goes a long way to gain loyalty and trust from people around you. How often have you thought about a supervisor or manager or even a teacher you had who was "tough but fair"? That's probably the person from whom you learned the most and certainly the one you most respect.

- **Consistency**—Moodiness will sabotage your success as a coach. People need to know that you are consistent in your expectations of them as well as of yourself.

- **Flexibility**—It's been said that supervisors and managers do things right, and leaders do the right thing. Doing the right thing in the right situation means that you have to be flexible and use your judgment in making a decision. You have to adapt your coaching style to the individual and the situation.

- **Resourcefulness**—Good coaches know how to get things done. They have the ability to draw on a variety of resources to aid in the coaching process. If they don't know the answer, they know whom to ask or where to go for help.

- **Empathy**—Good coaches have the ability to put themselves in the other person's shoes. They remember what it was like to learn a new task. Or they know what it means to feel inadequate in certain aspects of the job.

Supervisors and managers do things right; to be effective leaders they must do the right thing.

In addition to these qualities and traits, coaches need to develop the following skills and abilities:

- Communicating effectively
- Listening
- Questioning
- Setting goals and objectives
- Establishing appropriate priorities
- Analyzing
- Planning and organizing

We will address these skills as we look at the coaching process step-by-step.

Take a Moment . . .

Go back over the list of qualities and skills and highlight those you believe you already have. Then identify those you would like to develop further.

Qualities and skills I already have:

_____

_____

_____

_____

_____

_____

Qualities and skills I would like to develop:

_____

_____

_____

_____

_____

Modeling Coaching Behavior

In addition to traits and skills, effective coaches need to demonstrate certain behaviors. You can use the acronym COACH as a handy way to remember some of the most important behaviors: **C**ollaborate, **O**wn, **A**cknowledge, **C**ommunicate, and **H**elp. As we review the behaviors in detail, try to relate each one to yourself and your own situation.

- **Collaborate—The coaching relationship is a collaborative one.** Work with the staff member to identify the performance problem, set performance objectives, and develop a performance-improvement plan. Good coaches think in terms of how WE solve the problem.

- **Own—Examine your own behavior and accept some ownership for the problem.** Ask yourself: "Did I make my expectations clear?" "Did I provide the proper training?" "Does the staff member have the appropriate tools to do the job?"

- **Acknowledge—Acknowledge staff achievements as well as problems, feelings, and concerns.** The last point can be a challenge. Acknowledging problems and concerns is not the same as overlooking them or excusing unacceptable behavior or performance. For example, you can certainly acknowledge a staff member's difficulty in juggling the multiple responsibilities of both home and work. However, you cannot accept the resulting chronic absenteeism or tardiness.

- **Communicate—This is probably the most important behavior and the one many correctional supervisors and managers seem to find the most difficult.** As we noted earlier, communication skills, including listening, questioning, and giving and receiving feedback are critical for success. Coaches need to practice two-way communication on a daily basis and clarify expectations regularly.

- **Help—As a correctional supervisor or manager, you are not only a coach but also an advisor.** You serve as a resource person and a guide to other resources, both inside and outside the organization. In addition to giving help, you should also be seeking help from your staff. For example, if you need to implement a new procedure, ask your staff to help you develop a plan. At the very least, solicit their ideas. You will be surprised at how creative and innovative people can be when you give them a chance.

Leadership Series

Summary

Making the change from traditional correctional supervisor or manager to coach will require a commitment of your time and energy. You must develop new qualities, skills, and behaviors and improve communication with your staff. However, the benefits you and your staff will enjoy in improved performance, morale, and productivity will make your investment a worthwhile one.

Chapter One Review

Answers may be found on pages 102–103.

1. True/False. An annual performance appraisal can take the place of regular coaching.

2. Match the situations below with the type of treatment they require:

   A. Coaching
   B. Training
   C. Counseling

   ___ Chronic tardiness or absenteeism
   ___ Meeting only minimum standards
   ___ New responsibilities

3. Define the term coaching.

   _____

   _____

   _____

   _____

4. List four reasons why correctional managers and supervisors can be poor coaches.

   _____

   _____

   _____

   _____

5. List two reasons why staff may be uncoachable.

   _____

   _____

6. List four benefits of coaching.

   _____

   _____

   _____

   _____

7. Which of the following is a barrier to coaching?

___ A. Having patience

___ B. Knowing how to coach

___ C. Believing staff should improve performance on their own

___ D. Spending adequate planning time

8. List eight traits of effective coaches.

_____

_____

_____

_____

_____

_____

_____

_____

9. Define the letters in the acronym COACH.

_____

_____

_____

_____

_____

Chapter Two

UNDERSTANDING TODAY'S STAFF MEMBERS

Chapter Objectives

After completing this chapter, you should be able to:

- Describe the correctional manager's or supervisor's role as a coach and motivator.

- Identify different approaches to motivating today's correctional staff.

- Create a plan to make delegation work for you.

Even the best correctional coach can't force a team or staff member to change his or her behavior—the motivation to change has to come from within the individual. But correctional coaches can create an environment that fosters motivation by helping staff see the **WIIFT** of behavior change: What's In It for Them. To do this effectively, supervisors and managers need to understand the nature of motivation and what staff hope to get from their work.

> **Staff need to see the W I I F T of behavior change:** What's In It for Them.

What Staff Want

Motivation is directly related to morale, that is, the attitude of individuals and groups toward their work, work environment, and the organization as a whole. Effective correctional supervisors and managers motivate their staff, offering them a variety of incentives and rewards.

Researchers often divide these into two categories:

1.   Maintainers
2.   Motivators

Maintainers are factors that must be kept at a satisfactory level in order for staff to maintain performance. They include the following:

- Working conditions
- Organizational policies
- Job security
- Pay and benefits
- Relationships with co-workers
- Supervision
- Status

True Motivators create an inner desire to work.

True motivators are the factors that create an inner desire to work by satisfying certain needs which are important to the individual. They include:

- Achievement
- Recognition
- Satisfying work
- Responsibility
- Advancement
- Growth

Before you begin to coach your staff, analyze your organization based on these two categories. Does it provide incentives that will motivate staff to make the changes you want them to make? If not, what can you do to improve the situation and create a positive motivational climate?

Supervisors and Staff: Different Perceptions

The list above suggests a number of rewards that correctional supervisors and managers may offer staff in order to maintain and improve performance. Yet supervisors and managers often misinterpret what their staff want and attempt to motivate them with rewards that the staff members simply do not value.

Take a Moment . . .

Take a moment and rank the following motivating factors in order, according to what is important to you.

_____ Full appreciation of work done
_____ Feeling of being in on things
_____ Empathic help with personal problems
_____ Job security
_____ Good wages
_____ Interesting work
_____ Promotion and growth in the organization
_____ Personal loyalty to staff
_____ Good working conditions
_____ Tactful discipline

Now go back over the list and identify the order you think your staff members would choose.

_____ Full appreciation of work done
_____ Feeling of being in on things
_____ Empathic help with personal problems
_____ Job security
_____ Good wages
_____ Interesting work
_____ Promotion and growth in the organization
_____ Personal loyalty to staff
_____ Good working conditions
_____ Tactful discipline

During the past 50 years, researchers have conducted several studies asking staff to rank rewards in terms of their importance or motivational value to staff. These rewards include:

- Full appreciation of work done
- Feeling of being in on things
- Empathic help on personal problems
- Job security
- Good wages
- Interesting work
- Promotion and growth in the organization
- Personal loyalty to staff
- Good working conditions
- Tactful discipline

After staff rank-ordered the rewards, their supervisors were asked to rank the same items according to how the supervisors thought their staff would rank them. In each study, what supervisors and managers thought was important to staff differed dramatically from what staff said was important to them.

Staff ranked job security and good wages near the middle. Yet supervisors believed their staff would put good wages and job security in slots one and two, respectively. For example, a study conducted by Kenneth Kovack at George Mason University, produced these ranks:

Motivating Factors	Supervisor	Employee
Full appreciation of work done	8	2
Feeling of being in on things	10	3
Sympathetic help on personal problems	9	10
Job security	2	4
Good wages	1	5
Interesting work	5	1
Promotion and growth in the organization	3	6
Personal loyalty to employees	6	8
Good working conditions	4	7
Tactful discipline	7	9

Notice that supervisors put "feeling of being in on things" as number ten, but staff ranked it among the top three!

These studies show that supervisors and managers are often totally wrong in predicting how their staff would rank the list. What are the implications for coaching? If they misinterpret what is important to their staff, correctional supervisors and managers will choose methods of motivation that are entirely off-base. For example, a correctional supervisor may believe that all staff are motivated primarily by money. So he tries to help staff get ready for promotions and hopes for improved performance in return. Much to his surprise, staff performance does not improve. What the supervisor does not realize is that there may be other factors that are more important to his staff.

Talk to your staff about what's important to them on the job and really listen to them.

Based on the above study, the supervisor in our example would have better luck if he tried a different approach. He should learn what his staff hope to accomplish on the job so that he can provide them with interesting work. He should express full appreciation for the work they do, especially when performance improves. He also should keep staff informed of what's going on in the organization so that they feel that they are in on things.

How can you find out what will motivate your staff to change behavior in a coaching situation? You could ask them to complete the previous assessment, but you might not get accurate data. The best way is to talk to your staff and really listen to them. They will let you know directly or indirectly what's important to them. For example, suppose you have a staff member who frequently asks you, "How am I doing?" or "Did you like the way I handled that situation?" That's a good indication he or she is motivated by recognition.

Motivating Different Age Groups

Motivating staff is complicated further by generational differences. More than ever before, today's correctional supervisors and managers find themselves managing several generations of people at once. And the factors that motivate each group differ considerably. For example, people born roughly between 1943 and 1960 have been influenced by the events of the '60s and '70s. Idealistic and moralistic, the baby boomers' primary motivators have been money and freedom. Those born between 1920 and 1942 were influenced by the Great Depression and believe strongly in the importance of security and loyalty.

The so-called "Generation X"—born during the years 1965 to 1979—were raised on computers, video games, and VCRs. These individuals are both realistic and cynical. They have grown up watching their "workaholic" parents spend 14 to 16 hours at work, foregoing family vacations—often only to find themselves tossed out after 25 years of loyal service to the organization. Forget loyalty. Generation Xers want what they want now. They're interested in rewarding challenges and are willing to work hard. Yet, unlike their parents, Generation Xers fiercely guard their personal and leisure time. Because many grew up in dual career or single-parent families, they are self-reliant and independent. They also are not as intimidated by authority figures as those in previous generations.

Take a Moment . . .

Think about your staff members who represent different generations. What motivates each group? How do they say or communicate what is important to them?

_____

_____

_____

Creating A Supportive Work Environment

With so many different factors affecting staff motivation, where does a correctional supervisor or manager begin? Creating a supportive environment is a good first step. Studies show that when supervisors and managers create a supportive, nurturing climate, staff do what they believe is expected of them. Supervisors and managers can create such a climate in several ways:

1. Expect the best from staff.

2. Develop a flexible supervision or management style.

3. Eliminate barriers to individual achievement.

If you create a supportive, nurturing climate, your staff will do what they believe is expected of them.

1. Expect the Best

When supervisors and managers create high performance expectations and communicate them, staff members work to meet them.

People of all ages want to do a good job. Children start school eager and enthusiastic, yet within a relatively short period of time, much of that exuberance fades. Staff bring the same positive attitude and motivation to the workplace. Have you ever heard anyone say, "I'm going to go to work today and do a bad job"?

Expectations of staff + way you treat them = helps staff succeed or fail

What a supervisor or manager expects of staff members—combined with the way he or she treats them—will help determine the success or failure of those people. In their landmark book *In Search of Excellence,* authors Peters and Waterman put it very succinctly: "Label a man a loser, and he'll start acting like one."

Take a Moment . . .

List four situations or people in your workplace that would require you to modify your supervision or management style. Next to each name, write how you would change your style when working with that person or situation.

1. _____ / _____

2. _____ / _____

3. _____ / _____

4. _____ / _____

---

2. Develop a Flexible Supervision or Management Style

Vary your approach to the:
• Staff Member
• Situation

How would you characterize your supervision or management style? Do you use the same approach in every situation? Many supervisors and managers pride themselves on treating everyone the same, but doing so can be dangerous. Staff members are individuals with individual needs. Supervisors and managers should treat everyone fairly but not necessarily the same.

Supervising and managing flexibly also means varying your approach not only to the individual but also to the situation. A staff member who is new to the job will need more direction than a five-year veteran. However, if the veteran staff member is given a new task or responsibility, he or she may need more direction in that particular situation.

3. Eliminate Barriers to Individual Achievement

Identify a staff member who is not performing as you would like. Ask yourself if there is a barrier to that person's achievement which you have not previously considered. Many people who are labeled "failures" or "incompetents" are simply being hindered by relatively minor obstacles that supervisors and managers have not recognized. The tragedy is that after a while the staff members may begin to accept the failure label as fact.

Staff need the training, information, tools, and equipment to do the job.

When confronted with a staff member who is not working up to standard, ask yourself: Does the person have the knowledge and skills to do the job? If not, it's your job to provide him or her with the necessary training. Does the person have the appropriate tools? If not, get them. Make sure that people have the training, information, tools, and equipment to do the job.

Reward, Recognition, and Reinforcement

Reward, recognition, and reinforcement go hand-in-hand with motivation, but many correctional supervisors and managers still use old-fashioned, ineffective methods of rewarding staff. Some supervisors and managers try to inspire achievement with the carrot-on-the-stick approach, using incentive programs and promises of rewards. Others penalize negative behavior by wielding the symbolic whip. This type of supervisor or manager might say: "If you don't start getting to work on time, you'll be fired," or "You'll never get ahead if you continue to make these kinds of mistakes."

The problem with these methods is that they are short-term. Such quick fixes create no permanent behavior change. The next time, instead of a whip, the supervisor or manager will have to use a symbolic club to correct the staff member. Or the carrot that's being dangled will have to get bigger.

Think of rewards and recognition in terms of a flowering plant.

Rather than dangling carrots or wielding clubs, correctional supervisors and managers can use a more successful method. Think of reward and recognition in terms of a flowering plant. In order to get a plant to bloom, you must create the appropriate environment, using the right amount of light, water, temperature, and fertilizer. And if you have different types of plants, each will require different care. People are similar. The most successful reward systems make allowances for individual differences.

Simply offering encouragement is an important first step in the recognition process. Correctional supervisors and managers can develop a sense of competence and confidence in others by encouraging them to:

- acknowledge their own accomplishments, and
- strive toward their personal best.

Point out improvements in performance, no matter how small. This is particularly important when staff are beginning new tasks. As the German philosopher and poet Goethe once said, "Correction does much, but encouragement more; encouragement after censure is as the sun after a shower."

Encouragement and reinforcement need to be followed with recognition and rewards. Individual recognition teamed with incentive programs can be very effective. But they should be tied to organizational goals and consist of something that will be valued by the staff. For example, suppose your organization is committed to responding quickly to the public. Then you should reward staff members who are efficient in returning phone calls or resolving complaints.

The most successful reward systems make allowances for individual differences.

Any reward should be tailored to the person receiving it. The staff member with young children may appreciate being given more scheduling flexibility. However, someone on a limited income might value the opportunity to work overtime. Other reward possibilities include public recognition, time off, staff opportunities for training, or attending professional conferences.

Summary

There are many ways that correctional coaches can create a workplace in which staff will be motivated to make behavioral changes. And there are many ways that supervisors and managers can reward staff for their efforts. The secret to success is to learn what motivates your staff and what types of rewards and recognition they value. Listen to your staff; learn about their preferences and what they hope to gain from their work. Then create an environment in which each one can reach his or her highest potential.

Chapter Two Review

Answers appear on pages 104–105.

1. Define and list three maintainers and three motivators:

    _____

    _____

    _____

    _____

    _____

    _____

2. List the three top rewards identified by staff in several studies.

    _____

    _____

    _____

3. True/False. Today's younger workers want pretty much what their parents and grandparents wanted from their jobs.

4. List three factors that can help correctional supervisors or managers create a supportive work environment.

    _____

    _____

    _____

5. True/False. Different staff members require different types of rewards and recognition.

6. True/False. The carrot-and-stick or club approach is an effective reward system.

7. True/False. Staff and supervisors usu-
    ally agree on what's important to staff.

8. Why should you think of reward and
    recognition in terms of a flowering
    plant?

    _____

    _____

    _____

    _____

    _____

    _____

Part II

The Coaching Process

We have seen what coaching is and how staff motivation is necessary for coaching to succeed. We will now look at the steps of the coaching process.

The coaching process can be broken into three main segments:

- Planning and preparation

- Conducting the coaching session

- Action-planning and follow-up

Within each part are a number of individual steps, as illustrated by the flowchart on the next page.

We will consider each of those steps and the skills necessary to successfully complete them in Chapters Three through Six. In Chapter Seven, you will have the opportunity to create an action plan to develop your own coaching skills.

The Coaching Process

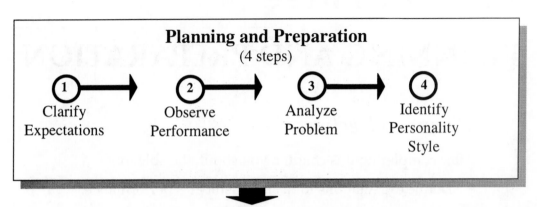

Planning and Preparation
(4 steps)

1 Clarify Expectations → 2 Observe Performance → 3 Analyze Problem → 4 Identify Personality Style

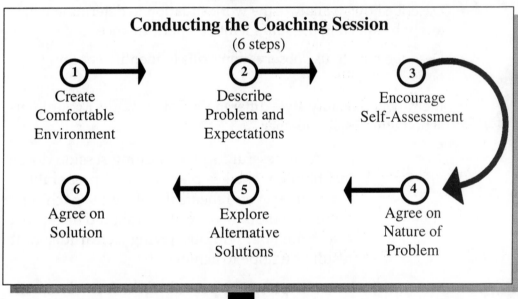

Conducting the Coaching Session
(6 steps)

1 Create Comfortable Environment → 2 Describe Problem and Expectations → 3 Encourage Self-Assessment

6 Agree on Solution ← 5 Explore Alternative Solutions ← 4 Agree on Nature of Problem

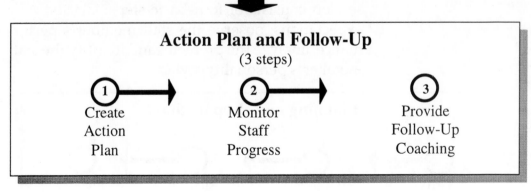

Action Plan and Follow-Up
(3 steps)

1 Create Action Plan → 2 Monitor Staff Progress → 3 Provide Follow-Up Coaching

Chapter Three

PLANNING AND PREPARATION

Chapter Objectives

After completing this chapter, you should be able to:

- Define expectations for a staff member's performance.

- Describe how to analyze the work situation to determine what might be affecting the staff member's performance.

- Describe how to use observation skills to identify coaching needs.

- Identify personality style differences that may affect your interaction with a staff member.

A successful formal coaching session doesn't just happen. It takes planning and preparation—sometimes even rehearsal. Informal coaching requires forethought as well. You should never coach a staff member without having a clear idea of the result you hope to achieve.

The planning process for a formal coaching session consists of four basic steps: Clarify your expectations, observe the staff member's performance, analyze the problem, and identify the staff member's personality style.

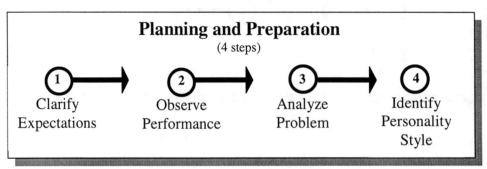

Planning and Preparation
(4 steps)

| 1 Clarify Expectations | 2 Observe Performance | 3 Analyze Problem | 4 Identify Personality Style |

① Clarify Expectations

Before you begin to work with the staff member, you will need to clarify your expectations for that person's performance. As you consider what you would like him or her to do, you may be tempted to think in terms of attitude or general qualities.

"I want Hamilton to show a more positive attitude."

"Brad needs to be better organized."

But statements like these will not give your staff the information they need to improve performance. What exactly should Hamilton do to show a positive attitude? How can Brad be better organized?

Instead of focusing on internal qualities like attitude or general tendencies like neatness, state your expectations in terms of behaviors—specific, observable actions that can be measured. For example, suppose you want a staff member to project a positive attitude toward his or her job. You would identify the behaviors that are a part of that—coming to work on time, treating offenders fairly, cooperating with other staff, and so forth. Describe specifically what kind of behavior you want—or don't want—a staff member in the position to demonstrate.

Take a Moment . . .

Rewrite the following statements so that they focus on behavior rather than attitude or general qualities.

1. Jamison is incompetent.

   _____

2. Hanson is sloppy in his work.

   _____

3. Tom just isn't interested in his job.

   _____

4. Joan is rude to the public.

   _____

Take the time to make a list of the performance behaviors you hope the staff member will change. Do this before you begin your session so that you will be ready to discuss them. Below is a sample list for Sidney, a clerical worker who is having trouble with word-processing.

My Expectations for Sidney's Performance

I would like Sidney's word-processing to be:
- Completed on time.
- Free of typing errors.

---

② Observe Performance

How does the staff member's current behavior differ from the behavior you would like to see? To find out, you will need to observe the staff member's performance. Try to be as objective as possible, focusing on the behaviors that are causing the performance problem—not on your reaction to or evaluation of the situation. As you record your observations, keep the following guidelines in mind.

- **Focus on specific behaviors that can be measured and changed:**
  "Jesse was late three times last week."
  "All of Miller's documents had at least five errors."

- **Don't just make note of what the staff member is doing wrong.** Keep track of what the staff member is doing right so that you can build on his or her strengths during the coaching session.

- **Determine the priority of the behaviors that the staff member needs to improve.** Don't try to work on everything at once. Select the behaviors that are most important for his or her success, and concentrate on those first. You can work on other behaviors in future coaching sessions.

Add your observations of current performance to your previous list of expectations for the staff member's behavior.

Sidney's Current Performance

Last week, I observed Sidney:

- was a day late typing the security alert memo and two days late with the State Compliance Report

- had several errors in each of those documents, plus errors in three other documents

Aspects of Sidney's behavior I would like to reinforce:

- greeted all visitors with a smile

- was patient with a difficult caller

- has set up an effective filing system

Priority of behaviors I would like Sidney to improve:

- meet all deadlines

- eliminate errors

Take a Moment . . .

Think about the staff member you indicated in Chapter One. What are your expectations for that person's performance?

_____

_____

What is the person's current behavior? What exactly does the staff member do that you want him or her to do differently?

_____

_____

What does the person say or do that you want him or her to continue?

_____

_____

Is there more than one behavior that needs to be changed or improved? If so, rank them in order of importance.

_____

_____

③ Analyze the Problem

As you compare your expectations for a staff member's performance to what that person is currently doing, analyze the situation. Determine what factors might be affecting the staff member's performance and whether coaching is the appropriate solution. You can do this by asking yourself the following questions:

- **What aspects of the staff member's performance are unsatisfactory?** Using your expectations for performance as a benchmark, identify the ways in which the current performance falls short.

- **Is it worth my time to coach in this situation?** Coaching is an investment of your time as well as the staff member's. Does the staff member have other problems that will keep him or her from benefiting from the process? Is the performance so poor that full-scale training or counseling is needed?

- **Does the staff member know my expectations?** Does the person fully understand what is expected of him or her?

- **What obstacles are there to meeting those expectations?** Are extenuating circumstances preventing the staff member from doing his or her best? Possibilities might include lack of proper training, too few resources, unrealistic standards, or too many other responsibilities.

- **What negative or positive consequences follow performance?** Does the staff member have any motivation to change his or her behavior? What can you do to stimulate that motivation?

- **Could the staff member change if he or she wanted to?** Does the staff member have the ability to do the job? After all, "ducks don't climb trees." Do you have a duck in a situation that requires a cat? Sometimes the problem is that we simply have someone in the wrong job. Coaching can't solve all your personnel problems!

As you prepare for your coaching session, prepare a list of answers to these questions, as in the following example:

Analysis of Sidney's Word-Processing Performance:

- **Was it unsatisfactory?**
  Yes, Sidney did not meet deadlines and had a high rate of errors. Projects should be error free and on time.

- **Is it worth my time?**
  Yes, Sidney performs his other tasks well.

- **Are my expectations clear?**
  I make deadlines clear to Sidney and point out typing errors.

- **Are there obstacles to meeting them?**
  Sidney has had some training on the word-processing software, but he might need more. I should ask him if he knows how to use the spell-check and macro features and make arrangements for further training if he does not.

- **Consequences of performance?**
  If Sidney's word-processing doesn't improve, he could lose his chance for promotion.

- **Could Sidney change if he wanted to?**
  Sidney has learned to do new things in the past; he should be able to master the word-processing software.

Of course you will need to talk with your staff member to learn if your initial assumptions are correct. Keep an open mind as you coach, and encourage your staff member to share his or her perspectives with you. You may learn some surprising and useful things about your organization.

Take a Moment . . .

Think about the staff member with a performance problem whom you identified on
page 38. Could any of the preceding reasons
be the cause of this person's performance
problem?

☐ Performance short of standards

☐ Counseling needed

☐ Obstacles in the way (If so,
    identify them)

☐ In the wrong job or assignment

☐ Other reason:

---

④ Identify the Staff Member's Personality Style

You have determined which behaviors you
would like to see change and the factors that
might be causing the problem. Now you need
to plan how to present this information to the
staff member. In order to do this effectively, you
will need to identify your staff member's personality style and adapt your coaching session
to that style.

People's personalities can differ in any number of ways; however, psychologists have identified four basic categories of personality styles.
Different personality models have given different names to each of the four styles. In this workbook, we will call them candid, persuasive, logical, and reflective. Although everyone possesses
traits from each style, each of us usually has one
style that is dominant.

Our style differences can get in the way of effective coaching, because we often relate to the other person in our own style instead of his or her style. When that happens, it's almost as though two people are speaking a different language. To increase your coaching effectiveness, you need to adapt your coaching sessions to the personality styles of your staff.

The first step to adapting to your staff members' personality styles is to identify your own. Read each of the following sets of questions and check the one in each set that is most like you. After you've read the section on interpreting your score, go back over the questions and try to imagine how your staff members would respond.

Personality Self-Assessment

1. When I am in a learning situation, I like to:
   __A. Be involved in doing something.
   __B. Work with people in groups.
   __C. Read about the information.
   __D. Watch and listen to what is going on.

2. When I am working in a group, I like to:
   __A. Direct the discussion and activity.
   __B. Find out what other people think and feel.
   __C. Remain somewhat detached from the rest of the group.
   __D. Go along with the majority.

3. When faced with a conflict situation, I prefer to:
   __A. Confront the situation head-on and try to win.
   __B. Work with the other person to arrive at an amicable resolution.

    __C. Present my position by using logic and reason.

    __D. Not make waves.

4. In a conversation, I tend to:

    __A. Come straight to the point.

    __B. Draw others into the conversation.

    __C. Listen to what others have to say, then offer an objective opinion.

    __D. Agree with what others say.

5. When making a decision, I tend to:

    __A. Make a decision quickly and then move on.

    __B. Consider how the outcome will affect others.

    __C. Take time to gather facts and data.

    __D. Consider all possible outcomes and proceed with caution.

6. I am seen by others as someone who:

    __A. Gets results.

    __B. Is fun to be with.

    __C. Is logical and rational.

    __D. Is a calming influence.

7. In a work environment, I prefer:

    __A. To work alone.

    __B. To work with others.

    __C. Structure and organization.

    __D. A peaceful atmosphere.

Now count the number of items checked for each letter. The letter with the most checks indicates your preferred personality style.

	Number
A—Candid	_____
B—Persuasive	_____
C—Logical	_____
D—Reflective	_____

As you read the brief descriptions below, determine for yourself the accuracy with which the description reflects your personal style.

Candid

Candid individuals are direct and controlling. They like to be both in charge and the center of attention. They are action-oriented and may be perceived as pushy and domineering. They enjoy being challenged, and they tend to make decisions quickly, sometimes with little information. Those with a candid style are demanding of themselves and others.

To be more effective, the candid person needs to be more sensitive to others, practice active listening, and exercise more caution in making decisions.

> **Coach the candid staff member by getting directly to the point.**

You can increase your effectiveness in coaching the candid person by quickly coming to the point during the coaching session. Because the candid person is often a poor listener, you will need to clarify and confirm frequently. Be sure to ask the staff member to summarize the discussion at frequent intervals. It is also important to give the candid staff member lots of recognition and reinforcement and challenge him or her with more responsibility and authority.

Persuasive

Those whose primary style is persuasive love people. They are outgoing, warm, and animated. They are very sociable and may be perceived as overly emotional. They have a short attention span and dislike details. Persuasive individuals are spontaneous, entertaining, and like to take risks.

To be more effective, the persuasive staff member needs to improve organizational skills and spend more time looking at the facts.

You can increase your effectiveness in coaching the persuasive person by creating a friendly environment. Take time at the beginning of the session to build rapport. Focus on the "people side" of the performance problem and appeal to the staff member's concern for others as a motivation for behavioral change.

Logical

Logical individuals pride themselves on their use of analysis and reason in all situations. They have a strong need to be right, and they rely on facts and data to support their position. Although they are good problem-solvers, they are slow to make decisions. They are sometimes perceived as aloof and critical. They often ask probing questions and frequently take the opposing point of view in a discussion.

To be more effective, the logical person needs to: be more flexible; spend less time gathering data; show more concern for people; and be more expressive of his or her feelings.

You can increase your effectiveness in coaching the logical person by using logical analysis. This helps the staff member identify the cause of and the solution to the performance problem. Recognize this person's need for detail and for the reasons behind your suggestions. Present your suggestions in a logical, step-by-step process.

When coaching a "logical" staff member, present your ideas in a logical, step-by-step process.

Reflective

Reflective individuals are reliable and cautious. They tend to be perfectionists and seek security. They avoid conflict and may be perceived by others as weak. Reflective people are good listeners and make great friends. They are loyal, cooperative, and supportive. For this reason, they are good team players.

To be more effective, the reflective person should learn to be more assertive, less sensitive, and more willing to take risks.

You can increase your effectiveness in coaching reflective staff members by encouraging and reassuring them. Exercise patience, because reflectives often approach a change in behavior more slowly and cautiously than other types.

Understanding and adjusting to different personality styles will help you become a more effective coach. Your acceptance of others and willingness to adapt will also encourage them to accept and adapt to you as well, creating better relationships throughout your workplace.

Candid	Demanding of themselves and others Direct, action-oriented, in charge, controlling, center of attention May be perceived as pushy or domineering Enjoy challenge Quick decision makers, sometimes with little information
Persuasive	Very sociable, outgoing, warm, animated, entertaining, spontaneous May be perceived as overly emotional Love people Short attention spans Dislike details Risk takers
Logical	Always rely on analysis and reason Use facts and data to support position Strong need to be right Ask probing questions and take opposing point of view in discussions May be perceived as aloof and critical Good problem solvers Slow to make decisions
Reflective	Perfectionists Reliable, cooperative, loyal, supportive Cautious, seek security, and avoid conflict May be perceived as weak Good listeners Good team players

Summary

Formal coaching is never a quick fix—it takes time and patience to facilitate another person's behavior change. As you gain more coaching practice, you will find that what works well for one person may not work for another. You may have to use trial and error until you match the right methods to the right people.

Thorough planning is your first step to making that match. Your next step is to develop your coaching communication, which we will consider in the next two chapters.

Chapter Three Review

Answers may be found on pages 105–107.

1. List the three major parts of the coaching process.

   _____

   _____

   _____

2. In order to coach effectively, you should clarify your expectations for staff behavior (choose one):

   __A. At the beginning of the coaching process, before the coaching session begins

   __B. During the coaching session, as you talk to the staff member

3. List the four steps of the planning process for a formal coaching session.

   _____

   _____

   _____

   _____

4. What are three things on which you should focus when observing staff performance before a coaching session?

_____

_____

_____

5. What are three factors that might cause unsatisfactory performance?

_____

_____

_____

6. Match the following personality styles with their definitions:
   A. Candid
   B. Persuasive
   C. Logical
   D. Reflective

   ___ Uses analysis and reason in all situations.
   ___ Outgoing, warm, and animated.
   ___ Reliable and cautious; seeks security and avoids conflict.
   ___ Direct and controlling; likes to be the center of attention.

7. You should _____ your coaching session to the staff member's _____ style.

8. Your expectations should be stated in terms of _____ and be _____ , _____ actions that can be_____.

9. How do you effectively coach staff with the following personality styles?

Candid _____

_____

_____

_____

Persuasive _____

_____

_____

_____

Logical_____

_____

_____

_____

Reflective _____

_____

_____

_____

Chapter Four

CONDUCTING THE COACHING SESSION: BEGINNING THE SESSION

Chapter Objectives

After completing this chapter, you should be able to:

- Describe how to build rapport with the staff member during the coaching session.

- Describe the staff member's current performance and your expectations for improvement.

- Explain how to use questioning skills to involve the staff member in the coaching process.

- Explain how to use active listening skills to ensure two-way collaborative communication.

Once you have fully planned your coaching session, you're ready to conduct it. There are three key steps to beginning a successful coaching session: Create a comfortable coaching environment, describe the performance problem and your expectations for performance, and encourage staff self-assessment.

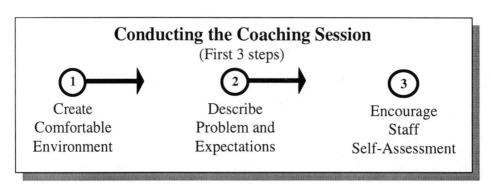

Conducting the Coaching Session
(First 3 steps)

1 ⟶ 2 ⟶ 3

| Create Comfortable Environment | Describe Problem and Expectations | Encourage Staff Self-Assessment |

① Create a Comfortable Coaching Environment

For a coaching session to be effective, the coach needs to create an environment in which the person being coached will feel safe and comfortable. You can do this by:

- Choosing an appropriate time and place for coaching.
- Establishing rapport with the staff member.

Choosing an Appropriate Time and Place

For your coaching session to succeed, both you and the staff member should be able to give each other your undivided attention. This often means scheduling a formal coaching session in advance. Whether your coaching session is formal or informal, choose a time when you are both relatively stress-free. To encourage open communication, select a location in which you can sit next to the staff member rather than across a desk. This usually means someplace other than your office. Look for a place without a lot of traffic, where you can speak privately. If you will need access to a piece of equipment, such as a computer, be sure it is available.

Establishing Rapport

Avoid jumping right in with an evaluation of the staff member's performance. Instead, begin your coaching session by establishing rapport and clearly stating the purpose for the meeting. For example, after asking the person how he or she is, you might say something like: "What I would like to discuss with you today is how I can help you be more successful in dealing with offenders who refuse to participate in their treatment programs."

Support your friendly approach with non-verbal communication. When the person speaks, sit forward in your chair to indicate interest. Avoid nervous gestures such as playing with your glasses or tapping your pen. Also avoid crossing your arms or leaning back with your hands behind your head. By crossing your arms, you can inadvertently send out a message that you're defensive. Similarly, leaning back with your hands behind your head and stretching is a demonstration of superiority—behavior that may put your staff member on the defensive.

You should not only be conscious of what you are communicating nonverbally but also of what the staff member is communicating nonverbally as well. For example, if the person is fidgeting in the chair, there's a good chance that he or she is nervous or uncomfortable with the discussion. Look for these cues and do your best to put the person at ease.

② Describe the Performance Problem

After creating a comfortable climate and putting the staff member at ease, you're ready to start the coaching session. Begin by describing the performance problem you identified in your observation of the staff member, and compare his or her current performance to your expectations. Remember to state the problem in terms of the behaviors you observed rather than trying to evaluate the person's attitude or emotional state.

Describe the staff member's performance in precise, objective terms.

Your coaching will be most effective if you describe the staff member's performance in precise, objective terms. Use the notes that you took as you observed the staff member to help you specify such features as:

Speed—(rate)
Quantity—(number or amount)
Accuracy—(absence of errors)
Thoroughness—(completeness)
Timeliness—(ability to meet deadlines)

Here are some examples of correctional coaches who provide specific descriptions of performance problems in relation to expectations:

"I've noticed that your visits to parolees' work sites have been down for the past six months. The average is 60 per month, and you've been ranging between 20 and 30."

"I'd like to talk with you about the number of errors you've been making in figuring employee time and attendance. During the last pay period, we had to refigure attendance for five employees. Our payroll procedures need to be free of this type of error."

"We've talked before about the importance of taking accurate counts. You've had three incorrect counts this week."

Expressing empathy can be useful at this stage. You might begin by saying, "I understand that it can be difficult for you to...but I expect...."

"This morning, I heard you shout at two different inmates who came to you with complaints. I know inmates are difficult to deal with, but our staff are always expected to speak in a normal tone of voice."

Take a Moment . . .

Using the staff member you identified at the beginning of the workbook as a case example, describe the current behavior—including the situation and the person's actions. Remember to be as specific as possible and focus on behavior, not attitude.

_____

_____

_____

③ Encourage Staff Self-Assessment

Staff will be more willing to participate actively in the coaching session if they have a chance to describe their own side of the situation. Before you continue with more detailed feedback, give the staff member a chance to evaluate his or her own performance. Hearing the person's perspective also will help you. It gives you a chance to determine what extenuating circumstances could be affecting his or her performance. In addition, it will give you a chance to verify those circumstances you might have noted earlier in your preparation process. This will help you decide whether coaching is really the best solution for the problem.

In order to help your staff express themselves during this part of the coaching session, you will need to develop two sets of skills:

- Questioning skills
- Active listening skills

Questioning Skills

Some staff members may be hesitant to offer their own ideas about their performance. One very effective way of getting people to open up is to ask open-ended questions—those that require more than a *yes* or *no* answer. Open-ended questions start with the words, *who, what, where, when, why,* and *how.* By asking questions that begin with *What thoughts have you given to . . . ? How does that fit into . . . ? What is your understanding of . . . ?* you will foster two-way collaborative communication.

Questions starting with *why* (*Why did you decide to . . . ?*) should be used with caution because they risk coming across as challenging and may cause the other person to become defensive. On the other hand, questions that begin with *Tell me more about . . .* can encourage someone to expand his or her comments.

> **Open-ended questions foster two-way collaborative communication.**

Take a Moment . . .

In order to unearth any underlying problems or extenuating circumstances, make a list of open-ended questions you can ask your staff member. After you list your questions, brainstorm some possible explanations for performance problems this person might give you. Of course, when you actually coach this individual, be aware that you might hear things you hadn't anticipated. Keep your mind open to other possibilities.

_____

_____

_____

Active Listening Skills

To be fully effective, a correctional coach's open-ended questions must be paired with active listening techniques. Many supervisors and managers fail in their coaching efforts because they spend most of their time in a coaching session talking. They tell staff member's how to handle a situation differently instead of asking questions and really listening to the person. This inability of supervisors and managers to listen isn't surprising. Although listening constitutes 45 percent of our communication activity, most of us listen at only a 25-percent level of effectiveness.

Listening = 45% of our communication; effective listening = 25%.

Listening Versus Hearing

Perhaps one reason why so many people are poor listeners is that they confuse *listening* with *hearing*. Hearing is the physical part of listening in which your ears sense sound waves. Listening, however, involves interpreting, evaluating, and reacting. Effective listening involves:

- Taking in information from the sender or speaker without judging.

- Clarifying what we think we heard.

- Responding to the speaker in a way that invites the communication to continue.

Correctional coaches can develop a number of *active listening techniques* that will help them achieve these goals:

- Listen to the staff member without allowing distractions to interfere with the listening process.

- Clarify and confirm what the person said.

- Reflect on his or her underlying feelings.

- Invite further contributions from the person.

- Discuss the implications of his or her statements.

- Probe to uncover the reasons why a situation exists and determine what should be done about it.

Listen Without Distraction

When a staff member speaks during a coaching session, give that person your undivided attention. Many things compete for our attention when we are listening. You may be distracted by noise from somewhere. Or, you may be trying to decide how you'll respond to the person's comments after he or she is finished. Block these from your mind and focus on what the other person is saying. You can determine your own response when he or she is done speaking. Instead, show the other person that you're listening. Maintain eye contact while he or she speaks. Wait until the other person is done talking before you respond.

Give the staff member your undivided individual attention.

Clarify and Confirm

When we listen, we interpret the speaker's message and then respond according to what we think he or she said. But often, our interpretations of that message are incorrect, and our responses can create misunderstandings and even conflict. It is important, therefore, to *clarify what we think* the speaker has just said by using some of the following approaches:

"As I understand it, what you're saying is . . . "

"What I hear you saying is . . . "

"I get the impression that . . . "

By paraphrasing the content of the message, the speaker can either confirm or further clarify the message, thus ensuring the accuracy of the communication.

Reflect Underlying Feelings

Listen for attitudes, feelings, and motives behind the staff member's words. Be alert to facial expressions, movements, gestures, and tone of voice. Confirm your perception by saying the following:

"If that happened to me, I would be . . ."

"I can imagine that you must feel . . ."

"You sound upset about the situation. Let's talk more about . . ."

Invite Further Contribution

When a staff member gives incomplete or short responses, the following will encourage him to expand on his points:

"Tell me more about . . ."

"I would like to hear your thoughts about . . ."

Discuss Implications

Sometimes you may be clear on what the other person said but uncertain about the statement's full implications. Often, this is a result of an incomplete message. To further clarify the speaker's intent, try to expand the discussion by using phrases similar to the following:

"If you did that, then you would be able to . . ."

"Would that mean that...?"

Probe to Uncover Reasons and Determine Next Steps

Asking more open-ended questions will help you discover the reasons behind a staff member's behavior. Further probing will also help you lead the staff member to ownership of the problem and a commitment to change. This type of questioning also supports the collaborative relationship.

"What prompted you to . . . ?"

"How can I help you . . . ?"

"Where do you think we need to focus . . . ?"

"When would be the best time to . . . ?"

"Why do you think he/she responded . . . ?"

Active listening is hard work, but it is well worth the effort. Active listening will result in more effective communication and more rewarding coaching relationships.

Take a Moment . . .

Visualize a coaching session with the staff member you identified on page 38. What questions or statements could you use to foster two-way communication?

_____

_____

_____

_____

_____

_____

_____

Take a Moment (*continued*)

For each category below, describe the statements or questions you could use to achieve active listening skills with a staff member.

Clarify and Confirm:

_____

_____

_____

_____

Reflect Underlying Feelings:

_____

_____

_____

_____

Invite Further Contribution:

_____

_____

_____

_____

Discuss Implications:

_____

_____

_____

Probe to Uncover Reasons and Determine Next Steps:

_____

_____

_____

Summary

You will make progress by successfully completing these opening steps of the coaching session. You and your staff member will be able to engage in an open dialogue about the performance problem in question. In the next portion of the coaching session, you will build on this open communication. You will collaborate with the person and generate a solution to the problem and an action plan for implementing it.

Chapter Four Review

Answers appear on pages 108–109.

1. List the three steps for beginning a successful coaching session.

   _____

   _____

   _____

2. True/False. Coaching can be done any time, any place. Just pick a performance problem and jump in.

3. When you describe a performance problem, you should state the problem in terms of _____ rather than _____.

4. When developing rapport, you must be conscious of what _____ and the _____ are _____ nonverbally.

5. True/False. Staff members will be more willing to participate actively in a coaching session if they have a chance to describe their own perspective on the performance problem.

6. What six words can be used to begin open-ended questions?

    _____

    _____

    _____

    _____

    _____

    _____

7. Distinguish between *hearing* and *listening*.

    _____

    _____

    _____

    _____

8. List three active listening techniques.

    _____

    _____

    _____

Chapter Five

CONDUCTING THE COACHING SESSION: DEVELOPING SOLUTIONS

Chapter Objectives

After completing this chapter, you should be able to:

- Describe how to help the staff member acknowledge the nature of the performance problem and his or her role in it.

- Describe how to use indirect communication to encourage staff member involvement in the coaching process.

- Explain how to join the staff member in exploring alternative solutions to the problem.

- Describe how to use feedback to provide the staff member with information that he or she can use to generate a solution to the problem.

- Explain how to achieve agreement on a solution to the problem.

In the remaining portion of the coaching session, you and the staff member will work together to decide what should be done about the performance problem. To do this, you will need to complete the following steps: Agree on the nature of the problem and the staff member's role in it, explore alternative solutions, and agree on a solution to the problem.

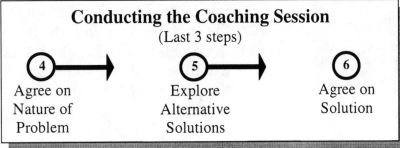

Conducting the Coaching Session
(Last 3 steps)

4 → Agree on Nature of Problem

5 → Explore Alternative Solutions

6 → Agree on Solution

④ Agree on the Nature of the Problem

For coaching to be successful—and to determine whether it is needed at all—you and the staff member must agree on the nature of the performance problem and his or her role in it.

Some staff members already will be aware of the problem and quickly agree with your initial description of it. But others may see the situation differently. They may not believe that a problem exists, or they may believe that other people are responsible for it. Give these staff members the opportunity to express their views. Listen with an open mind. Do you agree with their assessment of the situation? If you do, then take it into account as the two of you try to solve the problem. Perhaps coaching isn't the best solution to this problem at all. If you think the problem lies outside the staff member, then it might be a good time to arrange for further training or some other option.

If you don't agree with the staff member's view of the situation, you will need to provide more detailed feedback on performance. This will help him or her acknowledge the problem and take responsibility for it. The notes that you took during your observation of the person's performance will be especially helpful to convince the staff member that he or she has a performance problem. Continue to describe what you have observed. Discuss the situation with the staff member until the two of you agree on the problem and the affect it has on the organization and others. You might also suggest that the person ask him- or herself: "To what degree might I be contributing to the problem?" as in the following example:

Gary:

Thanks for stopping by, Eric. I'd like to discuss a problem I've been noticing with your performance. You were late getting your inmate counts to me on the last four nights you were in charge. We need to get accurate security counts at all times. When I don't get figures from you, it upsets the whole security process.

Eric:

I don't know what you're talking about. I do my job.

Gary:

You were two hours late yesterday and at least an hour late the other days.

Eric:

That wasn't my fault. It's the correctional officers—they just don't get me the numbers fast enough.

Gary:

The other watch commanders are able to get their numbers in on time, and they're working with some of the same correctional officers. Can you think of anything you might be doing that could be contributing to the problem?

Eric:

I go in, I ask for the numbers. What else is there?

Gary:

Think about how you ask for the numbers. And what about deadlines? Do you clearly tell them when you need the numbers?

Eric:

I shouldn't have to. They know we're on a tight schedule.

Gary:

They know time is tight, but it always helps to specify. Can you see now how you could be contributing to some of the lateness problems?

Gaining agreement from your staff member at this point in the coaching is critical to success. For the coaching process to be effective, you and the person must collaborate on a solution to the problem. The staff member will have little motivation to participate if he or she believes the problem doesn't exist or is someone else's responsibility.

Take a Moment . . .

What did Gary do to help Eric take responsibility for his performance problem?

_____

_____

_____

Would the case study staff member you identified on page 74 agree with your description of his or her performance problem? What do you think his or her response would be to your initial description of the problem?

_____

_____

_____

_____

_____

_____

If you don't think that the staff member would agree that a problem exists, what would you say to convince him or her?

_____

_____

_____

_____

_____

_____

---

⑤ Explore Alternative Solutions

After you and the staff member have agreed on the nature of the problem, the two of you can explore solutions to it. As you begin this step, remember that coaching is a collaborative process in which you and the person must work together. You should be able to do this if you continue your dialogue by:

- Using indirect influence to encourage further participation and creative problem-solving from the staff member.

- Using feedback to provide the staff member with more information about performance that could help him or her generate a solution.

Encouraging Staff Participation

You may be tempted to use your direct influence with the staff member and simply tell him or her how to solve the performance problem. However, this would do both of you a disservice. In order to learn and grow, staff need to be active participants in the problem-solving process. Their involvement will lead to a better solution, which in turn will lead to better performance and improved productivity for your entire team.

Actively participating in the problem-solving process helps staff learn and grow.

So, avoid directly telling staff members what to do during the coaching session. Instead, to encourage the initiative, independence, and self-expression necessary for successful collaboration use indirect influence. Indirect influence consists of four basic techniques:

- Accepting feelings.

- Developing ideas.

- Giving praise and encouragement.

- Asking open-ended questions.

Accepting Feelings

Staff members may experience a variety of emotions during the coaching process. They may feel that they are being unfairly singled out or that management's expectations for them are unreasonable. To resolve their feelings and move toward a positive solution to the performance problem, staff must be able to express themselves during the coaching session. Coaches can help by giving staff the opportunity to voice their feelings and accepting the feelings that are expressed. Statements like, "I can imagine that what he said upset you," show staff that their feelings are accepted as legitimate and valid, as in the following example:

Staff Member:
Senior management has no idea what it's like to have a civilian yelling at you when you're just trying to do your job.

Coach:
I know it can be stressful when you're caught between our policies and satisfying the public. Let's think up some approaches that will make these situations easier for you.

Developing Ideas

Staff may not only have strong feelings about a situation but also very definite ideas about what is taking place. In order to maintain open communication, you need to listen to the staff member and help him clarify, build, and develop his ideas. This technique is similar to that used in active listening and involves such responses as, "Let me make sure I understand what you're saying," and "As I hear it, you're saying that ... ."

At times, you may disagree with the ideas the staff member expresses. You should still listen to and acknowledge them. The two of you can work out the differences through discussion.

> **Listen to the staff member and help him or her clarify, build, and develop his or her ideas.**

Staff member:

Some people are coming in late and leaving early, and the rest of us have to pick up the slack.

Coach:

So as I understand it, you're saying that some people aren't doing their fair share when it comes to taking over the shift. Can you describe any specific situations when this has happened?

Giving Praise and Encouragement

Many staff members lack confidence in their ideas and their ability to improve performance. By giving praise or encouragement, you can help a staff member overcome this lack of confidence. Nonverbal gestures like nodding your head or simple comments like "go on" can help a person see his or her ideas as worthwhile. Staff members who lack faith in their own abilities also may need more encouragement, as in the following example:

Staff member:

I'm having a hard time learning this new system.

Coach:

I know the new system is a challenge, but I'm sure you can do it. Remember, you learned the old system. It just takes some time to get used to a new way of doing things.

Asking Open-Ended Questions

Open-ended questions are as important at this point in the coaching process as they are at the beginning. Questions that begin with *who*, *what*, *when*, *where*, and *how* encourage the staff member to develop his or her thoughts. This, in turn, will lead the two of you to a more thorough, well-reasoned solution, as in the following example:

Staff member:
I don't think this plan will work.

Coach:
Let's talk about it more specifically. What aspect of it do you think is causing the problem?

Staff member:
The transportation costs are way too high.

Coach:
Okay, what are some alternative ways we could transport the inmates?

Avoiding Negative Responses

Just as certain words and phrases encourage staff members to speak freely, others discourage dialogue. They convey to the person that his or her opinion is not needed or valued. To support open, two-way communication throughout the coaching session, avoid these types of negative responses:

Warnings: *"If you don't...."*

Unsolicited advice: *"You ought to ...."* or *"If I were you, I would ...."*

Challenges: *"Why did you ...?"*

Patronizing: *"You'll get over it."* or *"You'll be okay."*

Devaluing experiences: *"You think you have it bad? When that happened to me ...."*

Devaluing emotions: *"You shouldn't feel that way."*

Helping Reluctant Staff

Sometimes during coaching sessions, staff will insist that their supervisors or managers provide them with a solution to a problem instead of generating one themselves. Remember, the coaching session is most effective when the staff member takes an active role in solving his or her own problem. If a staff member responds to your coaching efforts with "I'll do whatever you say." or "Tell me what to do." resist the temptation. Continue to ask open-ended questions that will encourage the person to engage in the problem-solving process.

Avoid
- **Warnings**
- **Unsolicited advice**
- **Challenges**
- **Patronizing**
- **Devaluing experiences**
- **Devaluing emotions**

Take a Moment...

Use indirect influence to respond to the following statements a staff member might make during a coaching session.

Staff member: *I don't know how administration expects me to get any work done when I've got ten different people demanding things from me at the same time.*

Coach: _____

_____

_____

Staff member: *The way I see it, the problem is that we've got some people in this place who don't pull their own weight.*

Coach: _____

_____

_____

Staff member: *I don't think I'll ever be able to get this new software figured out.*

Coach: _____

_____

_____

Providing Detailed Feedback

It's important for you to encourage the staff member to take an active role in solving the performance problem. It's just as important, though, for you to share any information you have that could help him or her. In your observations, you probably noticed aspects of performance about which the staff member is unaware.

Is the staff member doing something that causes delays or alienates co-workers without even knowing it? The only way the person can change that behavior is if you describe what you've observed. Did you notice a behavior that you'd like to see the staff member repeat? Let him or her know—most people appreciate positive reinforcement.

The reason for giving feedback is to help the staff member succeed in the future.

You may feel awkward about giving feedback to others, especially if you have received feedback that you thought was unfair or inappropriate. You can overcome your awkwardness by remembering that the reason for giving feedback is not to criticize the person for past mistakes. It is to provide information that will help him or her succeed in the future.

Be sure that your feedback is balanced. Never give critical feedback without also providing the opportunity to discuss how the performance can be improved. Also, don't focus solely on the negative. Give positive feedback as well. During your observation you should have "caught" staff doing things right. Let them know what you saw.

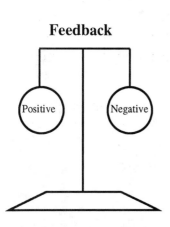

Feedback

Positive   Negative

Both positive feedback and critical feedback need to be specific. Just telling staff that they're doing a good job or that they need to improve is not helpful. It is much more effective and meaningful to say something like, "John, I liked the way you handled that difficult inmate. You showed a great deal of restraint and professionalism by not raising your voice or losing control."

Feedback Guidelines

Your feedback will be more effective and useful if you keep the following guidelines in mind:

- **Focus on behavior, not attitude.** Focus your feedback on the behaviors you have observed, not on the attitudes you think the person might hold. Instead of saying, "You never take your work seriously," try "Your last report contained several errors that needed to be reworked."

- **Be descriptive rather than evaluative.** Describe the behavior you have observed and its consequences without evaluating or passing judgment. Let the consequences speak for themselves: "When we have to rework errors, it takes longer and requires more effort to complete the process."

- **Be specific rather than general.** Describe behavior in the context of an actual situation: "I really liked the way you helped the new teacher, who was confused. Your directions were clear and easy to follow, and you took the time to draw him a map."

- **Discuss only behavior the person can change.** Be sure that the staff member is actually responsible for the behavior in question before you provide feedback on it.

- **Control your emotions and be sensitive to the staff member's emotions.** Giving and receiving feedback can be an emotional process, especially if you or the staff member are frustrated over the situation. Never raise your voice to a staff member or react out of anger, no matter how strongly you feel. If the person becomes upset, suggest that you take a break.

- **Communicate clearly.** Be sure that the staff member's interpretation of your words is accurate by asking the person to state his or her understanding of the discussion. Don't simply ask, "Do you understand?" This type of question is patronizing, and the person may answer "Yes" out of confusion or embarrassment.

Take a Moment . . .

You have a staff member who is always late, who turns in reports that are filled with errors, who completes the log poorly, and who frequently argues with other staff members. You are very frustrated with the situation. What feedback would you give this staff member?

_____

_____

_____

_____

Note: Don't let your feelings of frustration influence what you say to the person. Although the person's actions suggest that he or she cares little about the job, focus on behaviors rather than the person's internal motivation. Describe the situations you have observed and how they affect other people. Then ask the person for his or her perspective. Keep describing the implications of the situations until the staff member takes responsibility for correcting the problem.

Helping Staff Receive Feedback

Receiving feedback graciously and nondefensively is as much a skill as giving it. You may need to give your staff some tips to help them receive feedback with an open mind:

Receiving feedback graciously and nondefensively is as much a skill as giving it.

- **Develop a positive attitude toward feedback.** Look at feedback as an opportunity to collect important information that will help you become the person you wish to become.

- **Be prepared for feedback.** Make sure that when you ask for feedback, you are ready to accept it, even if it's critical. If you don't think you can deal with feedback at the time, wait until you are capable of handling it.

- **Don't get defensive.** It's human to become defensive when someone suggests we change our behavior. Remember, feedback represents one person's reaction to or perception of your performance. It has nothing to do with your overall abilities or your personal worth as an individual.

- **Check for understanding and clarification.** Use active listening techniques, such as stating, "Let me make sure I understand what you're saying," and paraphrasing what you think you heard. If the person giving feedback describes something in general terms, ask for specific examples.

Feedback is like a gift. And as with any gift, we thank the giver and then decide whether we want to keep it. Whenever you receive feedback, ask yourself if it has meaning and validity. Verify feedback by asking others if they share the same perceptions. You can collect different viewpoints, compare points of similarity and difference, and create a more objective picture of the situation. You can then use the information to either reinforce or modify your behavior accordingly.

⑥ Agree on a Solution

After you and the staff member have discussed the performance problem and alternatives for solving it, you will need to agree on a specific solution. As the two of you collaborate, keep in mind that your solution must be realistic and workable in order to succeed. State your solution in terms of behaviors that the person can perform. Those behaviors should be observable and measurable rather than expressions of attitudes or emotions.

You can help your staff member choose the best solution by:

• Asking open-ended questions to help the staff member identify possible barriers to enacting the solution. These can take the form of "What if ...?" questions:

Staff Member: *Jenkins is always willing to lend a hand. I think I could get it done on time if Jenkins would help me with the whole thing and not just the last part.*

Coach: *What do you think would happen differently if you asked Jenkins to do that?*

• Asking more questions to help the staff member generate strategies for overcoming those barriers. These questions should encourage the person to take a second look at situations:

Staff Member: *I know I could meet deadlines if I knew how to use the software better, but with three people sharing a computer, I never get a chance to practice.*

Coach: *Is there another computer you might be able to use a few times until you're up to speed?*

As you work with the person, you should also ask what you can do to help him or her make the solution a success. It may not be appropriate or possible for you to do everything the person asks; if that's the case, it's a good starting point for further discussion and negotiation. The person may even generate a better solution during your dialogue.

Role-Playing

As you and the staff member work toward agreement on a solution, role-playing can be a helpful tool. Role-playing can serve a variety of uses at this point in the coaching session, including:

- Helping the person see the effects of various solutions.

- Giving the person a chance to practice new behaviors and actions.

The following scenario illustrates how role-playing can be used in both ways:

Steve is coaching Ray on how to handle difficult inmates. The two of them have generated a number of alternatives and are now trying to choose the best approach. Steve takes the role of correctional officer and acts out the various approaches. Ray, playing the inmate, predicts the response. Once the two of them have identified the most effective approach, they switch roles. This gives Ray the chance to practice the approach before dealing with the next difficult inmate.

Case Study One: The Correctional Manager

As you read the following case study, ask yourself whether the parole manager is using the effective coaching techniques we've discussed so far. Are there things you would try to do differently if you were the coach?

Scenario: *Vera, a parole manager, has accompanied Dan, a new parole agent, on his worksite calls visiting parolees on the job. The two have called on four parolees that morning and five in the afternoon. It's near the end of the day. The* *manager suggests that they stop at a coffee shop for a debriefing session before they call it a day.*

Vera: *It's been a pretty exhausting afternoon, hasn't it?*

Dan: *Boy, I'll say! Some of these parolees can be really tough to motivate.*

Vera: *Well, that's what I want to talk to you about. I thought this would be a good opportunity to give you some feedback on what I observed and to give you some suggestions to help your calls go more smoothly. After all, both your goal and mine is to help you keep more parolees on the job. Right?*

Dan: *Absolutely. Okay, let me have it.*

Vera: *Let me start by saying that I think one of your biggest assets is that you are very warm and friendly. That really helps in establishing rapport with the parolee. You have a great personality, and you do a great job of connecting with the parolees.*

Dan: *That's good to know. I've been told that I have the gift of gab and can convince anyone to do anything.*

Vera: *You certainly have the talent. All we need to do now is to fine-tune those skills. One of the things you have going for you is that you seem to know the programs well. It's obvious that you're well-versed on the opportunities parolees have to get more help. You do a good job of getting the main points across in a very limited amount of time. Do you agree?*

Dan: *Absolutely. I'm really confident that I know the programs, and the opportunities.*

Vera: *Since knowledge is not a problem, we need to take a look at what is getting in the way of a* *really successful parolee call. The biggest thing I notice is that in your eagerness and enthusiasm, you aren't taking enough time to plan your parolee call. As a result, you come across as disorganized and unprepared. That's one thing. The second problem I see is that you seem to be a little too eager to convince the parolee to participate in one program opportunity instead of taking the time to analyze the situation. Do you know what I mean?*

Dan: *I'm not sure I do.*

Vera: *For one thing, you don't ask enough open-ended questions to uncover what the parolee's most important needs really are. Because you know the programs so well, you seem to focus on just telling the parolee about the program. I also think that you need to do a better job of really listening to what the parolee is telling you. I don't think you're picking up on the nonverbal cues. What I would recommend for your next set of calls is to do a better job of planning, including the preparation of some open-ended questions. During the call, concentrate on asking open-ended questions and really paying attention to the parolee's responses, including body language. Other than those few things, I think you're doing a good job. So, do you think you can work on these things?*

Dan: *Well . . . okay.*

Vera: *Good. I'm sure you'll see a big difference the next time out.*

Take a Moment . . .

Take a moment now to jot down those things you thought the coach did well and those areas in which you think she could improve. What did the coach do well?

_____

_____

What could the coach have done better?

_____

_____

Here are some points you might have listed:

What the coach did well—By accompanying Dan on calls to parolees, Vera was able to observe his performance. She analyzed what he was doing and compared it to her expectations for him. She took the time to build rapport at the beginning of the coaching session. She also took the time to point out aspects of Dan's performance that were effective as well as those things she hoped he would change.

What the coach could have done better—Vera identified two performance problems for Dan: that he appeared "disorganized and unprepared" and that he needed to focus more on the parolees' needs instead of just describing the programs. Her description of the first problem was too general to be useful. Instead of calling Dan disorganized, she should have described specific incidents from the calls: "In one call, you forgot the parolee's name, and in another, you were confused about the parolee's current program." She also didn't provide an opportunity to discuss how Dan might solve this first performance problem.

Vera provided more detail in her description of Dan's second performance problem. But she didn't give Dan much opportunity for self-assessment. He was never able to say whether he agreed with her view of his performance or not. He also didn't get much of an opportunity to ask questions about Vera's feedback.

Vera provided Dan with advice instead of allowing him to generate ideas for solutions. She did not even take the time to see that he fully understood her advice. Dan's statements "I don't know what you mean" and "I guess so" show his confusion. But she didn't pick up on it and offer him any further explanation. Vera also didn't ask Dan any questions to determine whether her solution to the situation was the best one. Dan really wasn't a full partner in this coaching session, and he will probably have some difficulty enacting the changes that Vera recommended.

Here are some different approaches Vera could have taken when describing Dan's performance problems:

Vera: *One thing I noticed during your calls is that you sometimes got confused when you were talking to the parolees. In one call, you forgot the parolee's name and in another call, you were confused about the parolee's current program. That type of thing can make the parolees feel that they aren't important to you. What do you think might be happening here?*

Dan: *I try to plan out all my calls before I make them. But sometimes I get so excited that I forget to look at my notes before I go into the office. I need to slow down and review my notes before I* *get out of the car.*

Vera: *That sounds like a good plan. Another thing I noticed is that you might be closing some of your calls too quickly instead of seeing if the parolees have other needs we can fill. Did you notice that both Adams and Rodriguez seemed interested when you mentioned the new AA meetings?*

Dan: *No, I didn't. How could you tell?*

Vera: *I watched their body language. Both of them leaned forward in their chairs and made direct eye contact when you started talking about new AA meetings.*

Dan: *If I'd noticed that, I could have told them where the meetings are held and at what times. I wish I knew more about body language. I'd pay more attention if I knew what to look for.*

Vera: *I have a book that might help you. I'll give it to you when we get back to the office. We can also do some role playing to help you practice.*

Summary

By engaging in open dialogue, Vera and Dan were able to collaborate on solutions to Dan's performance problems. The solutions were more effective than the ones Vera developed without input from Dan. Thus, he will be more motivated to follow through on a solution that he helped develop. The final phase in this or any coaching session is to:

- get the staff member's commitment to a specific action plan;

- carry out the solution and;

- set up follow-up sessions to monitor the staff member's progress.

We will discuss how to develop an action plan and conduct follow-up coaching in the next chapter.

Chapter Five Review

Answers may be found on pages 110–112.

1. List the steps for developing a solution with the staff member.

   _____

   _____

   _____

2. If you and the staff member you are coaching do not agree on the nature of the performance problem and the person's role in it, you should (choose one):

   ___ A. Give the person the opportunity to express his or her views.

   ___ B. Refuse to compromise your authority by listening to any of the person's arguments.

   ___ C. Ask your supervisor his or her opinion.

   ___ D. Verbally reprimand the staff member.

3. You and the staff member must_____ on a solution to the problem.

4. Indirect influence consists of these four basic techniques:

   _____

   _____

   _____

   _____

5. True/False. When providing feedback, you should describe what staff members are doing right as well as what they need to improve.

6. True/False. Role playing is not beneficial during a coaching session.

7. List four of the six guidelines for giving
   effective feedback.

   _____

   _____

   _____

   _____

8. Mark the following practices that should
   be used in a coaching session.
   _____Patronizing
   _____Unsolicited advice
   _____Praise
   _____Warnings
   _____Constructive criticism

9. To receive feedback with an open mind,
   one must:

   • Develop a _____ _____ toward
     feedback.
   • Be _____ for feedback.
   • Avoid getting _____.
   • Check for _____ and _____.

10. What two techniques can you use dur-
    ing a coaching session to help a staff
    member choose the best solution to a
    performance problem?

    _____

    _____

Chapter Six

ACTION-PLAN AND FOLLOW-UP

Chapter Objectives

After completing this chapter, you should be able to:

- Describe how to help the staff member develop an action plan for improving performance.

- Explain how to monitor the staff member's performance as he or she works to improve.

- Explain how to provide follow-up coaching as needed.

The final phase of the coaching process involves:

- Creating an action plan to put the solution you have agreed on into action.

- Monitoring the staff member's progress.

- Scheduling and conducting follow-up coaching sessions as needed.

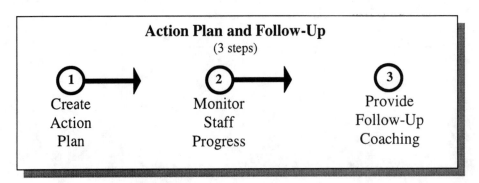

Action Plan and Follow-Up
(3 steps)

1 → Create Action Plan

2 → Monitor Staff Progress

3 Provide Follow-Up Coaching

① Create an Action Plan

You and the staff member have agreed on a workable solution. The next step is to ask him or her to outline a plan for putting the solution into action. You then ask the staff member to state it verbally. Developing an action plan will give the person direction for making the solution a reality. It will also help build the staff member's commitment to seeing the solution work. The plan can be simple, as in the following example.

Coach: *We've talked about some different ways you can avoid errors with your log entries. Could you review them for me?*

Staff member: *I'll read over each finished entry to be sure I didn't leave anything out and to be sure it's specific.*

Of course, many action plans will be more detailed than the above example. In these cases, ask the staff member to spell out deadlines for performing various actions and what the end result will be:

Coach: *Let's review exactly what you're going to do to get the accreditation report out on time and when you'll complete each step.*

Staff member: *I'll call the department heads at the same time and ask if I can have their reports in one week. That should give me a full week to work with those materials before the final report is due.*

You can use your questioning and feedback skills to help the staff member consider any obstacles that might keep the plan from succeeding. If you have agreed to do something to support the person's efforts, you should restate that as well:

Coach: *I'll let each of the department heads know how important it is to get the material to you on time.*

② Monitor Staff Progress and
③ Provide Follow-Up

You and the staff member have agreed on an action plan. Now the two of you should set up a time when you can meet and discuss the person's progress. This will give you the opportunity to monitor the staff member and provide any follow-up coaching that might be necessary. Schedule your follow-up far enough in the future that the person will have time to put the solution into practice. But be sure the follow-up is not so far off that he or she will begin to think that you've forgotten about the matter.

Preparing for Follow-Up

To prepare for your follow-up session, observe the staff member's performance. Is the person successfully making the changes that the two of you agreed on? Are there performance areas that could still use improvement?

Make note of what you observe, both the behaviors you want to reinforce and the behaviors that need further improvement. Record specific examples of each that you can share with the person during a follow-up session.

Follow-Up Coaching

Coaching is an ongoing process in which you and the staff member will strive for continual improvement. Your follow-up coaching session will give you a chance to provide your staff member with feedback on what you've observed about his or her performance. It will also give the staff member a chance to describe any barriers he or she may have encountered. Based on this information, you may continue to revise your solution until both of you are satisfied that the problem is solved.

You can also provide the person with informal follow-up coaching as you observe his or her performance. Informal follow-up coaching is most effective if done immediately after you have observed the behavior in question. For example, if you saw a staff member handle a difficult inmate successfully, you might wait until the inmate is gone and then say, "You handled that inmate well. Even though you couldn't give her what she wanted, you gave her a choice and let her make her own decision." Remember to never let informal coaching turn into a situation in which you take over and do the staff member's job. Even if the person is having difficulty, wait until the situation is over before you offer advice (so long as safety and security will not be jeopardized).

Take a Moment . . .

Using the staff member you identified on page 74 as an example, write down some ways you could monitor the person's progress. Remember, however, you are doing this in isolation. In the actual situation, the person would help determine the plan of action.

_____

_____

_____

_____

_____

_____

Case Study Two: Hold the Phone

By now you should be familiar with all the steps of the coaching process. Can you identify them in action? Read the following discussion between a corrections manager and a staff member. Then identify the steps the manager follows to coach the person to improve performance. At the end, you'll have a chance to evaluate the manager's coaching abilities and describe what you would have done differently.

Scenario: *Kurt, a training academy manager, must help Deana, the receptionist, come up with a better way to handle phone calls when trainees are in the reception area.*

Kurt: *Deana, come in and have a seat. I'd like to talk to you about a problem I've been noticing with your job performance.*

Deana: *What are you talking about? I've been doing my job okay.*

Kurt: *Yes, Deana, you perform your job duties very well. However, I want to talk with you about your interactions with people on the telephone. On four different occasions during the past two weeks, I've noticed that you allowed the telephone to ring at least six times before you answered it. When you finally did answer it, you told the callers to wait a minute. Then when you got back to them on the phone, you asked them what they wanted. But you didn't apologize for keeping them waiting. I have noticed this behavior on several occasions. What seems to be the problem from your perspective?*

Deana: *I don't think there is a problem. I get back to them as soon as I can. After all, there's only one of me. I often have other people in front of me that I have to take care of. What do you want me to do— ignore them?*

Kurt: *As we have discussed in our staff meetings, we are committed to providing the highest level of service to all of our trainees, both face-to-face and on the telephone.*

Deana: *Look, I'm doing the best I can. Maybe if you hired more people, we wouldn't have this problem. I can't do two things at the same time. Besides, if they don't want to hold, they can call back later. And I'm not the only one who doesn't answer the phone right away, but I don't notice you giving anybody else grief. Have you talked to Tom about it? He never answers the phone unless he has to.*

Kurt: *Let's keep in mind that we expect everyone to provide the best service to our trainees. And right now, we're talking about your performance. I understand that at times you are pulled in several directions at the same time. I did say that the trainees in front of you should take priority. However, the people on the telephone can't see that you have someone in front of you, and when the telephone rings and rings, the caller gets frustrated and angry.*

Deana: *So what do you want me to do?*

Kurt: *Deana, what do you think you could do to keep the trainee in front of you happy while responding to the incoming call?*

Deana: *I don't know. That's what I'm asking you.*

Kurt: *I suggest that you ask the trainee in front of you to excuse you for a moment and then immediately answer the telephone. Then ask the callers if you can put them on hold, or if they would like you to call back when you're free.*

Deana: *That's what I do now. I tell 'em to hold.*

Kurt: *Deana, there's a difference between telling them to hold and asking if they would like to hold.*

Deana: *What difference does it make? Nobody likes to be put on hold, so why bother asking?*

Kurt: *People like to be given options. They like to feel that they are making the decision.*

Deana: *Okay, fine. I'll do it. Is there anything else?*

Kurt: *Not really. Let's just make sure we're both clear on the action plan. Tell me what you are going to do differently in dealing with the callers.*

Deana: *I'm going to concentrate on answering the phone more promptly. And I will be friendlier and apologize for putting them on hold.*

Kurt: *Good. Let's get together again in two weeks to discuss how things are going. How does that sound to you?*

Deana: *Okay, I guess. I'll give it a try.*

Take a Moment . . .

Identify the various steps of the coaching process that you see in this interaction. (If you need a review, turn to the flowchart on page 33.)

Once you've identified the steps of the coaching process, make a note of those steps that you thought the coach executed well and those areas in which you thought the coach could improve. What did the coach do well?

_____

_____

_____

_____

_____

What could the coach improve upon?

_____

_____

_____

_____

Here are some points you might have noticed:

What the coach did well—Kurt did a good job of describing Deana's current performance with the telephone and citing specific incidents when Deana left callers on hold. Kurt invited Deana's self-assessment of the problem and kept her on the topic when she wanted to talk about other staff and their performance problems.

Kurt empathized with Deana's difficulty in being pulled in several different directions at once when dealing with trainees in person and callers on the phone. Yet Kurt did not buy into Deana's complaint that more staff were needed. Kurt made sure that Deana clarified an action plan for improving performance and stated exactly what the plan would involve. Kurt also set up a follow-up time for monitoring Deana's performance.

What the coach could have done better—Kurt didn't take time to build rapport with Deana at the beginning of the coaching session. Also, the abrupt mentioning of the performance problem put Deana on the defensive. Kurt might have received more cooperation from Deana by opening the coaching session this way:

Kurt: *Hi Deana, could you come in here a minute? How are things going for you in the reception area?*

Deana: *Fine, I guess. We've been really busy lately.*

Kurt: *I've noticed that. I've also noticed that we've been getting a lot of phone calls while trainees are in the reception area. I know it's difficult to juggle the phone when you have* *people in front of you. So I wanted to talk about some ways you could do that more effectively.*

Kurt also wasn't assertive enough in getting Deana to generate a solution to the problem. Although the two of them agreed on a solution, Deana had no part in creating it. Thus, she may not be motivated to make the behavioral changes to carry it out. Kurt might have gotten more involvement from Deana by encouraging her to think of the situation from a caller's perspective.

Kurt: *Deana, what do you think you could do to keep the trainee in front of you happy while responding to the incoming call?*

Deana: *I don't know. That's what I'm asking you.*

Kurt: *Put yourself in the caller's place. You've called places before and been put on hold. How does it make you feel?*

Deana: *I hate it. No one likes to be put on hold.*

Kurt: *Okay, so you don't like it. Why not?*

Deana: *It's a waste of time. You never know how long you're going to wait before someone can talk to you.*

Kurt: *What could the people on the other end do to make it easier on you?*

Deana: *Tell me how long it's going to take, for one thing.*

Kurt: *What if we tried that with our callers?*

Summary

We have seen that by following the steps of the coaching process you can help your staff members improve their performance. Through coaching, you can actively involve them in the problem-solving process. You can also encourage them to take responsibility for their own professional development and success on the job. This not only will improve productivity but also will increase job satisfaction and motivation.

Coaching is the correctional management technique of the future, and the sooner you begin to develop your coaching skills, the better. In the final chapter, you'll have the chance to create an action plan for putting the techniques you've learned in this workbook into practice.

Chapter Six Review

Answers may be found on pages 112–113.

1. List the key action words that identify the three steps of the final phase of the coaching process.

   _____

   _____

   _____

2. Creating an action plan can:
   ___A. Give a staff member direction for making the agreed-on solution a reality.
   ___B. Build staff commitment to seeing the solution work.
   ___C. Get the staff member to talk about his performance problems.
   ___D. Both A and B.

3. What can a coach do to prepare for a follow-up session with a staff member?

   _____

   _____

   _____

   _____

4. A follow-up session gives the coach a chance to:

   _____

   and gives the staff member a chance to:

   _____

5. True/False. Follow-up coaching can be formal and informal.

6. True/False. Coaching is a one-time process to correct short term performance problems.

Chapter Seven

DEVELOPING A PERSONAL ACTION PLAN

Chapter Objectives

After completing this chapter, you should be able to:

- Describe how to overcome obstacles to coaching.

- Explain how to evaluate your readiness to coach.

- Describe how to develop a plan for improving your coaching skills.

- Explain how to monitor and evaluate your success as a coach.

Preventing Coaching Pitfalls

There's no doubt that coaching takes time, patience, and practice. But the effort you put into developing your coaching skills will be richly rewarded. Coaching gets results. The organization benefits from improved staff performance, increased productivity and bottom-line results. Staff members benefit from increased self-esteem and job satisfaction. The correctional supervisor or manager benefits by meeting goals and objectives with less stress.

Coaching gets results.

As you begin to develop your coaching skills, you may find barriers to coaching within your organization. You may be one of the few people in your organization who is willing to take the time to coach. You may even work in an organization that does not reward or value coaching as a management practice. But don't give up. Effective coaching can only improve the performance of your team or department. And, when other correctional supervisors or managers see its effectiveness, you'll be on the way to creating a coaching culture within your organization.

Staff may initially resist coaching. Those who have never been given the opportunity to participate in decisions or use their own judgment may be suspicious. They may need reassurance that your efforts are sincere. Emphasize that you are trying to help them reach their full potential. Also emphasize that each staff member is responsible for his or her own professional growth and development.

Your Action Plan for Coaching

How will you develop your coaching skills? Just as you would require a staff member to develop an action plan to improve performance, use this opportunity to create one for yourself.

To improve my coaching skills, I plan to:

_____

_____

Action steps I will take to improve my coaching skills include:

_____

_____

Obstacles that may hinder my efforts to become an effective coach include:

_____

_____

Steps I will take to overcome obstacles include:

_____

_____

I will know I have succeeded in becoming a more successful coach when:

_____

_____

Measuring Success

One of the ways you can measure your coaching success is to solicit feedback from your staff. One easy and relatively risk-free method is to ask each staff member to complete an anonymous "agree-disagree" questionnaire, as in the following example:

Please indicate whether you agree or disagree with each statement. Please express your true feelings. Your responses will remain anonymous.		
My supervisor or manager:	**Agree**	**Disagree**
1. Frequently tells me how I'm doing.		
2. Gives me both positive and negative feedback.		
3. Tells me what he/she expects of me.		
4. Asks my opinion and involves me in decisions that affect me.		
5. Keeps me informed about changes taking place in the organization.		
6. Does not use threats or intimidation.		
7. Acknowledges my extra effort with some type of praise or recognition.		
8. Takes the time to explain new procedures and makes sure that I understand them.		
9. Provides the training and resources I need to do my job.		
10. Treats me with respect.		
11. Is not afraid to admit his/her mistakes or to say, "I'm sorry."		

Respond to the above list as you think your staff would respond. Are there any areas you would like to improve? Compare your self-perception with the perception of your staff—it could be a real eye-opener! Regardless of the outcome, you now have valuable data that reinforces the positive approach you already are using for identifying areas for improvement.

Note: If you choose not to give the questionnaire to your staff, discuss the statements with your supervisor. Ask for his or her feedback.

Summary

Effective coaching takes time, effort, and a real interest in and commitment to developing people. The investment is substantial, but the payoff is enormous.

Final Review

Review your understanding of the coaching process by answering the following statements. Answers appear on pages 113–114.

1. True/False. In a coaching session, the coach should speak for the majority of the time.

2. One of the most effective ways to encourage two-way communication is to ask _____ questions.

3. True/False. One of the coach's responsibilities is to help staff solve their own problems.

4. True/False. Coaching sessions should always be spontaneous and unstructured.

5. Every coaching session should end with both parties _____ on an action plan.

6. The purpose of coaching is to _____ behavior.

7. True/False. During the coaching session, the coach should refrain from overloading the staff member with too many points.

8. True/False. Performance appraisal time is usually the best occasion for coaching.

9. True/False. *Coaching* and *counseling* mean the same thing.

10. Coaching is an _____ process.

11. List the the steps of the coaching process in the diagram below.

The Coaching Process

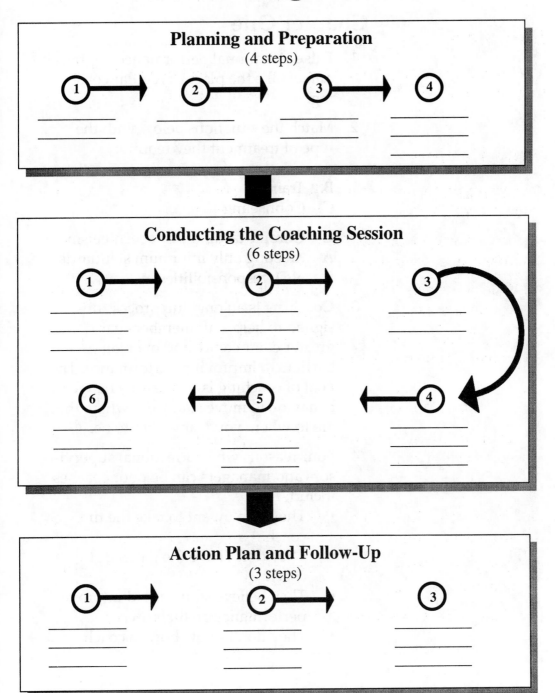

Answers to Chapter Reviews

Chapter One

1. **False.** An annual performance appraisal *cannot* take the place of regular coaching.

2. Match the situations below with the type of treatment they require:
   A. Coaching
   B. Training
   C. Counseling

   C Chronic tardiness or absenteeism
   A Meeting only minimum standards
   B New responsibilities

3. **Coaching** is an ongoing process designed to help staff members gain greater competence and overcome barriers to improving performance. The goal of coaching is to create a change in behavior, to move staff from where they are to where you want them to be.

4. Four reasons why correctional supervisors and managers can be poor coaches include:
   - They don't want to take the time to coach.
   - They don't have the patience to coach.
   - They believe staff should improve performance on their own.
   - They don't know how to coach.

5. Two reasons why staff may be uncoachable are:
   - They are resistant to change.
   - They think they know it all.

6. The four benefits of coaching are:
   - Coaching is the most effective way to develop your staff.
   - Coaching is the key to managing multiple priorities.
   - Coaching leads to improved staff performance.
   - Coaching increases staff's self-esteem and job satisfaction.

7. Which of the following is a barrier to coaching?
   A. Having patience
   B. Knowing how to coach
   √ C. Believing staff should improve performance on their own
   D. Spending adequate planning time

8. Eight traits of effective coaches are:
   - communicating effectively
   - listening
   - questioning
   - setting goals and objectives
   - establishing appropriate priorities
   - analyzing
   - planning
   - organizing

9. The letters in the acroynym COACH stand for:
   - **C**ollaborate
   - **O**wn
   - **A**cknowledge
   - **C**ommunicate
   - **H**elp

Chapter Two

1. **Maintainers** are factors that must be kept at a satisfactory level in order for staff to maintain performance. Maintainers include (choose three):
    - working conditions
    - company policies
    - job security
    - pay and benefits
    - relationships
    - supervision
    - status

    Motivators are the factors that create an inner desire to work by satisfying certain needs that are important to the individual. Motivators include (choose three):
    - achievement
    - recognition
    - satisfying work
    - responsibility
    - advancement
    - growth

2. The top three rewards identified by staff are:
    1. Interesting work
    2. Full appreciation of work done
    3. Feeling of being in on things

3. **False**. Today's younger workers want different things than their parents or grandparents did from their jobs. Younger workers are interested in rewarding challenges and are willing to work hard. But unlike their parents, they fiercely guard their personal and leisure time. They are self-reliant and independent. They also are not as intimidated by authority figures as those in previous generations.

4. Three factors that can help correctional supervisors or managers create a supportive work
   environment are:
   1. Expect the best from staff.
   2. Develop a flexible supervision or man-
      agement style.
   3. Eliminate barriers to individual achieve-
      ment.

5. **True.**

6. **False**. The carrot-and-stick or club approach
   are *not* effective reward systems because they
   do not produce permanent changes in behavior.

7. **False**. Studies show that supervisors and
   managers are often wrong in predicting what
   is important to their staff.

8. You should think of reward and recognition
   in terms of a flowering plant because both the
   plant and a person need the right things to
   grow. In order to get the plant to bloom, you
   must create the appropriate environment,
   using the right amount of light, water, temperature, and fertilizer. Each plant—like each
   person—requires different care.

Chapter Three

1. The three major parts of the coaching process
   are:
   1. Planning and preparation
   2. Conducting the coaching session
   3. Action-plan and follow-up

2. In order to coach effectively, you should
   clarify your expectations for staff behavior:
   √ A. At the beginning of the coaching process,
        before the coaching session begins
   B. During the coaching session, as you talk
      to the staff member

3. The four steps of the planning process for a formal coaching session are:
   1. Clarify expectations
   2. Observe performance
   3. Analyze problem
   4. Identify personality style

4. The three things you should focus on when observing staff performance before a coaching session are:
   1. Specific behaviors that can be measured and changed
   2. What the staff member is doing right as well as things that need to be improved
   3. The priority of the behaviors that the staff member needs to improve

5. Factors that might cause unsatisfactory performance include (choose three):
   • lack of proper training
   • too few resources
   • unrealistic standards
   • too many other responsibilities

6. Match the following personality styles with their definintions:
   A. Candid
   B. Persuasive
   C. Logical
   D. Reflective

   C. Uses analysis and reason in all situations
   B. Outgoing, warm, and animated
   D. Reliable and cautious; seeks security and avoids conflict
   A. Direct and controlling, likes to be the center of attention

7. You should **adapt** your coaching session to the staff member's **personality** style.

8. Your expectations should be stated in terms of **behaviors** and be **specific, observable** actions that can be **measured**.

9. How do you effectively coach staff with the following personality styles?

Candid
You can increase your effectiveness in coaching the candid person by quickly coming to the point during the coaching session. Because the candid person is often a poor listener, you will need to clarify and confirm frequently. It is also important to give the candid staff member lots of recognition, reinforcement, responsibility, and authority.

Persuasive
When coaching the persuasive staff member, create a friendly environment. Take time at the beginning of the session to build rapport. Focus on the "people side" of the performance problem and appeal to the staff member's concern for others as a motivation for behavioral change.

Logical
When coaching the logical staff member, use logical analysis. This helps the person identify the cause of and the solution to the performance problem. Recognize the person's need for detail and for the reasons behind your suggestions. Present your suggestions in a logical, step-by-step process.

Reflective
When coaching the reflective staff member, encourage and reassure them. Exercise patience, because reflectives often approach a change in behavior more slowly and cautiously than other types.

Chapter Four

1. The three steps for beginning a successful coaching session are:
   - Step 1—Create a comfortable coaching environment.
   - Step 2—Describe the performance problem and your expectations for performance.
   - Step 3—Encourage staff self-assessment.

2. **False.** Coaching should be done only after a proper coaching environment has been created.

3. When you describe a performance problem, you should state the problem in terms of **behaviors** rather than **the staff member's attitude or emotional state.**

4. When developing rapport, you must be conscious of what **you** and the **staff member** are **communicating** nonverbally.

5. **True.**

6. The six words that can be used to begin open-ended questions are: *who, what, where, when, why,* and *how* (use cautiously to avoid putting the person on the defensive).

7. **Hearing** is the physical part of listening in which your ears sense sound waves. **Listening** is interpreting, evaluating, and reacting to what is said.

8. Active listening techniques include (choose three):

- Listening to the staff member without allowing distractions to interfere with the listening process.
- Clarifying and confirming what the person said.
- Reflecting on his or her underlying feelings.
- Inviting further contributions from the person.
- Discussing the implications of his or her statements.
- Probing to uncover the reasons why a situation exists and determining what should be done about it.

Chapter Five

1. The steps for developing a solution with the staff member are.
   - Step 4—Agree on the nature of the problem and the staff member's role in it.
   - Step 5—Explore alternative solutions.
   - Step 6—Agree on a solution to the problem.

2. If you and the staff member you are coaching do not agree on the nature of the performance problem and the person's role in it, you should (choose one):

   √ A. Give the person the opportunity to express his or her views.
   B. Refuse to compromise your authority by listening to any of the person's arguments.
   C. Ask your supervisor his or her opinion.
   D. Verbally reprimand the staff member.

3. You and the staff member must **agree** on a solution to the problem.

4. Indirect influence consists of these four basic techniques:
   - Accepting feelings
   - Developing ideas
   - Giving praise and encouragement
   - Asking open-ended questions

5. **True.**

6. **False**. Role playing *is beneficial* during a coaching session because it:
   - Helps the person see the effects of various solutions
   - Gives the person a chance to practice new behaviors and actions

7. The guidelines for giving effective feedback are (choose four):
   - Focus on behavior, not attitude
   - Be descriptive rather than evaluative
   - Be specific rather than general
   - Discuss only behavior the person can change
   - Control your emotions and be sensitive to the employee's emotions
   - Communicate clearly

8. The following practices should be used in a coaching session:
   Patronizing
   Unsolicited advice
   √ Praise
   Warnings
   √ Constructive criticism

9. To receive feedback with an open mind, one must:
   - Develop a **positive attitude** toward feedback.
   - Be **prepared** for feedback.
   - Avoid getting **defensive**.
   - Check for **understanding** and **clarification**.

10. The two techniques you can use during a coaching session to help a staff member choose the best solution to a performance problem are:
   - Ask open-ended questions to help the staff member identify possible barriers to enacting the solution.
   - Ask more questions to help the staff member generate strategies for overcoming those barriers.

Chapter Six

1. The key action words that identify the three steps of the final phase of the coaching process are:
   - Creating
   - Monitoring
   - Scheduling and conducting

2. Creating an action plan can:
   A. Give a staff member direction for making the agreed-on solution a reality.
   B. Build staff commitment to seeing the solution work.
   C. Get the staff member to talk about his performance problems.
   √ D. Both A and B.

3. What can a coach do to prepare for a follow-up session with a staff member?
   - Observe the staff member's performance.
   - Make note of what he or she observes—both positive and negative behaviors.

4. A follow-up session gives the coach a chance to **provide feedback on what he or she has observed about the staff**

member's performance and gives the staff member a chance to **describe any barriers he or she may have encountered in trying to improve performance.**

5. **True.**

6. **False**. Coaching is an **ongoing process** in which **you and the staff member** will strive for **continual improvment**.

Final Review

Answers to the coaching process questions:

1. **False.** A coach should have the ability to **listen** to as well as talk with the staff member.

2. One of the most effective ways to encourage two-way communication is to ask **open-ended** questions.

3. **True.**

4. **False.** Coaching can be either spontaneous or planned.

5. Every coaching session should end with both parties **agreeing** on an action plan.

6. The purpose of coaching is to **change** behavior.

7. **True.**

8. **False.** Coaching should be done throughout the year.

9. **False.** Coaching is designed to help the staff member gain greater competence at work. Counseling is directed at personal issues that are affecting performance.

10. Coaching is an **ongoing** process.

11. The coaching process:

The Coaching Process

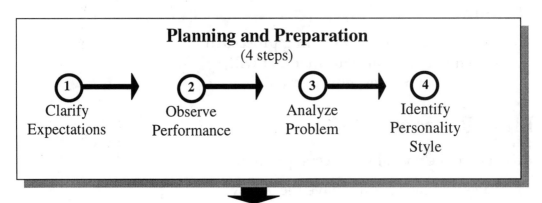

Planning and Preparation
(4 steps)

1. Clarify Expectations
2. Observe Performance
3. Analyze Problem
4. Identify Personality Style

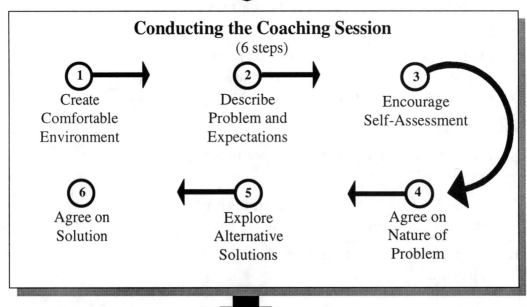

Conducting the Coaching Session
(6 steps)

1. Create Comfortable Environment
2. Describe Problem and Expectations
3. Encourage Self-Assessment
4. Agree on Nature of Problem
5. Explore Alternative Solutions
6. Agree on Solution

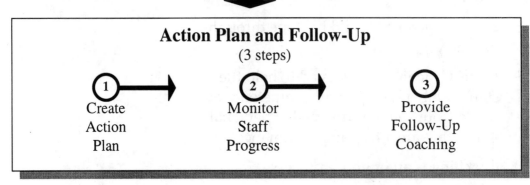

Action Plan and Follow-Up
(3 steps)

1. Create Action Plan
2. Monitor Staff Progress
3. Provide Follow-Up Coaching